After Death Signs

from

Pet Afterlife & Animals in Heaven

How to Ask for Signs & Visits and What They Mean

Brent Atwater

the Animal Medium

Brent Atwater's
Just Plain Love® Books presents

Copyright information © 2008-2018 by B. Brent Atwater
Published and Distributed in the United States by:
Brent Atwater's Just Plain Love® Books
www.BrentAtwater.com

Editorial: Brent Atwater   Cover Design: Brent Atwater
Interior Design: Brent Atwater   Illustrations: Brent Atwater

Library of Congress Cataloging-in-Publication Data

Paperback ISBN: 1514355612
ISBN-13: 978-1514355619
Hardcover ISBN:
EBook ISBN: 9781310851612
Kindle: ASIN: B01628P7WE
Audio:
Translated into multiple languages.

Visit Brent Atwater's web site
www.BrentAtwater.com

Dedication

This book is written to honor my entire inspiring and
beloved canine, feline, equine and other animal teachers,
guardians and companions (including "Fishy") with whom
I shared my experiences, learning and life.
From my heart and soul to yours, thank you! My special love
goes to each and every one of you
for filling my life and heart with joy.

To Thomas Michael Ramseur Wellford,
whose life, love and passing made my understanding possible.
I shall always hold you and hear you in my heart,
my soul and my dreams.To those very special people and fur
babies who are my joy, and with whom I share hope, laughter
and LIFE!!!

Acknowledgements

I want to thank you the reader for taking the time to explore my Just Plain Love® Books and for allowing me to share what I have learned and am learning about pet loss, death, pet life after death, pet reincarnation and animal communication through other individuals and my personal experiences.

Special thanks to Michael Wellford and my precious fur, finned and feathered companions for their contributions and enduring patience with me and my spiritual path.

It is my intent that this information will facilitate inspiration, provide comfort, support, greater perspectives and answer your questions through expanded awareness in your life.

I thank those who have supported and encouraged my journey and the authors, speakers and teachers who contributed to shaping my consciousness.

My gratitude also goes to each individual who has shared their story with me so our readers can derive hope and be inspired by "all that is."

A special thank you to all pets, animals and their guardians who's NEVER ending love bond represents why I write my books.

This *Just Plain Love*® **Book**
is given
To: _____

Message: _____
Date: _____
with
LOTS of LOVE, HUGS and KISSES!!!

From: _____

& **"Friend"**

TABLE OF CONTENTS

I want to say

If you are reading this introduction you're probably an animal lover or someone you know needs a GREAT BIG HUG!

I want to thank all God's wonderful and cherished creatures who have taught me what I share with you in this book that I write to honor all their lives.

I have written in a conversational manner and chose not to be limited by strict traditional editing to enhance the emotional connections. Writing is an art; I'm allowed that creative expression.

This book derives its information from over 20 years of research and my communications gathered over decades. The stories about Signs, Messages and Visitations are the embodiment of lessons pet parents learned and how their heart's awareness evolved to a higher consciousness through experiencing each after death messages, sign and lessons imbued by their deceased pets.

It is my intent that this book comforts you, reassures your Soul's knowing and helps ignite hope, in addition to providing healing insights and answers to questions that expand your awareness to all things possible and real!

These true examples will probably give you tingles and goose bumps (a friend calls them God bumps) of confirmation. I hope you can relate to the thoughts, feeling and experiences of each pet parent and perhaps think
Hummmmmm, that relates to what's going on in my life!

If someone has told you
"it's just a pet, he's dead, get over it." This book will
prove them wrong!

It will guide you to understand and have profound
new experiences!
You will learn to embrace your beloved animal
companion's insights, signs, connections and
communications from the Other Side and
KNOW it's real!

Brent Atwater's
Just Plain Love® Books presents

Brent Atwater how do you know about Signs, Visitations & the Other Side?

In 1997 on Friday evening my fiancé Mike called at 6:30 pm to say he would be home at 9:30 pm. He was killed in a head-on collision.
My world was shattered!

Life as I knew it was **over**!

I grieved excessively and uncontrollably for years. Where was he, how could this happen and WHY??? I vowed to find answers and to be able to connect and communicate with him. To survive,
my heart **had to have** answers!

When I screamed, "why won't you let me know you're OK?" From the Other Side Mike quietly said, "If you'll stop crying so hard, I'll show and teach you how to connect and communicate with me." My learning journey began.

My investigation into death, afterlife and life after death became my life's mission because I desperately wanted to find Mike. I started researching ways that his energy could connect with, communicate and return to me.

Mike, in Spirit form, began teaching me how to connect and communicate with him. I pass these lessons forward to you in this book. His death also activated my Gifts to see and talk face to face with deceased Spirits.

Can a Pet's life (energy) continue beyond Death?

Many folks think about and "sorta" believe this concept.
I **know** this is real!!

Prepare to expand your awareness and understand the **concept of Transition.** This book provides compelling evidence and testimonies that Animal Life after Death is REAL.

Then you can move into "good grief" to heal your Heart.

Let's get started!

the Dog with MY "B" on His Bottom!

What led you to research Deceased Pets and the Other Side?

For years Pet Spirits have been after me to write this book. They want you to know they're alive and well and CAN and WANT to connect with you.

So, as They say to me "listen up!"

While studying life after death I became more and more aware that my dogs demonstrated similar if not downright exact character traits of each other.

"Friend" my red border collie was born with a white "B" on his bottom that exactly matches my signature. I took that as my Sign to write about what my heart learned from Mike's transition- that life after death communication and connection with the Other Side and Reincarnation is real for pets too!

Each pet testimonial validated and illustrated before and after death communication and provided proof that dead pets live on in Pet Spirit form as they continue to interact with and be an ongoing part of our lives on Earth.

I started my global Facebook Pet Group so no one can say I "made this stuff up!" –plus people worldwide could ask questions and have discussions about pets and the Other Side. I learned many people want to understand and experience After Death connections with their beloved pet. Why? Because it helps heal their heart!

Please visit my other resources listed in the back of this book.

FYI

My favorite thing is answering questions. You can Find Q & A events on my YouTube Channel, Radio Shows, Facebook Brent Atwater Live Page, my Pet loss group or in Personal Readings.

For more information go to www.BrentAtwater.com

Physical Death is the Beginning of a NEW journey thru the Transition process. The Pet's soul vacates its fur suit and changes immediately into a living energy form that comes back to you as a Pet Spirit or a "Comeback Kid"! How do I know? I see your pet's energy transition and watch this process.

Each biological body provides several opportunities (exit points) to separate the Soul's energy from the physical body it resides in. When that body ages, is physically broken or ill, just wears out or the Soul decides to opt out early during birth or the newborn process, it's all part of just changing energy forms.

A Soul's energy NEVER dies, it just changes forms!

Due to shorter life spans, upgrading to a healthier body is a necessity for our beloved animals, birds, fish or reptiles so they can continue sharing your life's journey, whether in "steam" / Spirit form or as a reincarnated pet.

Like Humans, animals have multiple exit points that they can choose to use to leave. That's why "when its time," you and your pet inherently understand what's going on. It's a script you both agreed to for this exit point and learning opportunity. No matter how gentle or horrific your pet's transition is, remember, you and your pet chose this specific scenario to enhance each soul's growth.

If you are reading this book prior to the impending passage of the "love of your life," know that shedding the Earth suit through Transition is the FIRST step in reuniting with you.

Death is NOT forever, it's just FOR A WHILE!

Those factual words will help you during Transition and the waiting process. It will save you a lot of tears

while waiting in anticipation of what their new
Living energy form will be, rather than being
engulfed in prolonged grief that "he is Dead".

Death is NOT forever,
it's just FOR A WHILE!

Animal Reincarnation Animal Afterlife Book by Brent Atwater

Energy is Never Ending!

If you boil WATER, what does it make? STEAM
If you freeze STEAM, what does it become?
ICE CRYSTALS! If you melt ICE CRYSTALS,
what does it become? WATER!

It's the law of physics! Energy never dies. Think about the water- ice- steam concept! The energy base of water never goes away; it just changes into different physical forms.

Did you know that the human body is made up of about 75% water and a cat's body about 60%? According to the ASPCA water makes up to 80 % of your dog's body weight.

You might want to think of a pet that has left his original body i.e. shed his pet suit as being in "steam" or "sparkler" form at the Rainbow Bridge.

Then he chooses to be continuing Living energy as a Pet Spirit or takes on another physical form ("pet / earth suit") for a return trip.

The never-ending living energy cycle is continuously changing into different energy formats and physical FORMS.

A Soul's Energy NEVER changes!
It just changes into different physical FORMS.

© Animal Reincarnation Animal Life After Death by Brent Atwater

Brent Atwater's
Just Plain Love® Books presents

The Transition Process

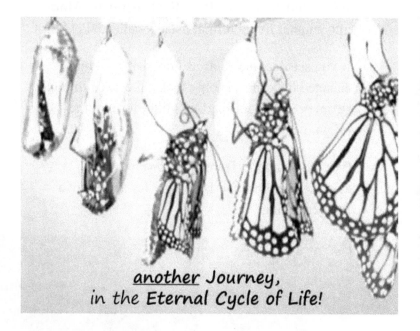

another Journey,
in the Eternal Cycle of Life!

Why do you use the word Transition?
The word Transition is factually correct according to
Physics and is softer and gentler than "put down",
death and put to sleep or euthanized. During the
death process a pet's energy **does transition** out of
its Earth "pet suit" to Heaven or "all there is" in the
Universe.

As the physical body (scaled, finned, feathered or fur suit) is left behind the Pet's Soul energy transforms into another living format usually called a Pet Spirit.

If you see deceased pets as I do, that Soul now changed into Spirit energy looks like a see-through steam or iridescent sparkler glitter form of the original pet.

By embracing the Transition concept, you acknowledge that energy never dies and is not a forever ending.

During the Transition process, your pet's physical body will be in conflict with its Soul's love for you. His Soul will want to stay on Earth to emotionally support you through his vacating the fur suit, although every soul understands that's not possible.

When a pet is preparing to pass over and you subliminally want them to "hang on" for your sake:
*The pet will walk away or distance themselves from you,
*Not look at you in your eyes,
*Avoid their normal personal contact habits,
*Stay or hide in another room trying to avoid the conflicting energies.

Another sign of impending Transition is when you see an older or sickly pet sitting at a window or door just staring out as if they are memorizing their last earthly view.   They are!

Cat Spirits want you to know
"from the moment I transitioned
my Love for you is Eternal...

Let's continue our Never Ending Love Story!"

After Death Signs from Pets Afterlife & Animals in Heaven
Book by Brent Atwater   © Dianne Virga Photographer

Signs that Physical Transition is Imminent

Usually 24 – 48 hours prior to leaving its body/ fur
suit/ shell, your pet's Soul will start to withdraw its
life force energy. If you can see energy, their aura
will gradually diminish and draw closer to the body
instead of radiating outward. During that time or
beforehand you can ask your pet if it is going to
reincarnate.

If you see Auras (a field of subtle, luminous outside
of the body radiation surrounding a person, pet or
object like a halo), you will be able to notice your
animal's electromagnetic life force energy (aura)
becoming more centrally organized near the heart
area. During that time an animal's physical body

becomes colder as their energy is being incrementally withdrawn in preparation for departure. This progressive physical process starts as cold paws and ears, pale gums, then lackluster or nonresponsive eyes, etc.

If you see animal's life force energy, you can watch an animal also draw his aura energy **inside** of his body. As that process initiates, your pet's aura will begin to start getting lots of black holes in it. When the pet's aura energy surrounding the body becomes totally black, at that time, you know their Soul's life force energy has completed transition, detached and exited from its body.

You will then see whirling purple energy (that's THE highest Spiritual energy) rotating in an upward counter clock wise direction as their life force essence rises up to cross the death line, a solid black area, before reappearing on the other side as a bright white Sparkler form.

Do not have any guilt about the death/ Transition process. It's a Process, **NOT** a Dead end! Whatever occurred was "scripted" and agreed upon between your souls before it happened. Your pet knew and knows he was/ is loved and that you were/are doing the best you could/can do. If the Transition was "an accident" that scenario was planned too. Your Pet is perfectly whole, healthy and healed the nano second they become a Pet Spirit.

Again- Everything is EXACTLY as it should have been with your pet's transition for the lessons, gifts and learning opportunities you each contracted to experience.

How to Assist a Pet's Transition

The Affirmation below will assist your cherished companion in transitioning easier and without horrific physical complications.

1. Hold its front paws/feet with your hands or place the hand that you write with (that's your energy sending hand) on the pet's body near its heart. If this is difficult to do it's not imperative.

2. Look into your pet's eyes if possible but not necessary. Ask within your heart or voice out loud: (Say one time or as often as you wish.)

Affirmation to Assist Pet Transition

"Fill in blank with Pet's name, I love you.
I honor, respect and support your choices.
From the love in my heart, I send you my life force
energy to use **as you so choose**."

It is imperative that you use the words
"as you so choose" so your pet can use that
additional energy boost to either cross over or to get
better.

Then it's THEIR choice! Your pet can choose to
survive and stay at this exit point or cross over.

**Do not change the wording or it will change the
type of energy sent**. Your intent will assist in
making your pet's transition to another dimension as
gentle as possible.

Remember, no matter what **you** desire, there is a
point beyond which any physical body cannot
regenerate or recover.

* MOST IMPORTANT: Pet Loss is **NOT** pet death.
Pet Loss is about **loss of the Pet Earth suit** and
TRANSITION into living energy i.e. Pet Spirit form!

To learn more, subscribe to my YouTube channel for answers explaining transition, signs, afterlife, animal life after death, animal health, communication and healing. We have LOTS of Archives. I'm sure there's a video addressing your concerns. If not, let me know!

To help heal your heart, my radio show "Alive Again" on www.PetLifeRadio.com has Podcasts that are available 24/7 with lots of Archives.

What is a Memory Moment?

After Transition, you will be grasping for anything to honor the special bond you shared with your pet. At some point in time before your Pet transitioned, they created a tender precious *Memory Moment*. It's their way of acknowledging and honoring the love between you as they complete that particular earthly

41

lifetime. At first, during deep grief you might not recognize it, but in hindsight it will become a vivid and cherished *Memory Moment*!

A *Memory Moment* is an action or behavior that is out of character for the way your pet normally behaves or has been acting.

Example: one pet sat and stared deeply into it owner's eyes for several days before he passed. Another pet would lie on the other side of the terrace trying to distance their energy from their pet parents. Our Pet Loss Radio Show on Pet Life Radio.com "Alive Again" has several great podcasts archived on this subject. Get your Kleenex ready.

A *Memory Moment* is also your pet's way of letting you know that everything is Ok- no matter what happens and **that he KNOWS what's going on** and that he **will be and is fine** after finishing the Transition process!

A great example …. A client's cat was extremely ill and stayed alone in a dark corner in her bed for months. Several days after the client started saying the Transition Affirmation on p 38, her cat got up, came over to sit in her lap and purred for the first time since her illness began. Later that night she calmly went to sleep (unassisted) in the safe haven of her owner's love while her guardian was stating that Affirmation. What a wonderful *Memory Moment*!

Can a Pet come back in multiple life times
Yes, that's called reincarnation?

The belief in reincarnation has been embraced by the world's largest and oldest religions for over 6,000 + years. That fact says something! If you believe in past lives, then subliminally you believe in reincarnation because you have to have a past life to reincarnate! If you don't subscribe to this concept it's perfectly ok and will not affect any after death communication and Signs from your deceased Pet.

However, until you open your mind to the possibility of their return, your pet will not come back / reincarnate. Why? Because they will honor your belief choice. An open mind facilitates the return of your pet more readily.

Disbelief creates an energetic barrier, like a closed mind stops learning opportunities. However, if you choose not to believe that pets can come back and you and your pet have scheduled a return in this lifetime, the Universe will provide many situations to assist you with an "opportunity" to change your mind to complete your spiritual agreement.

On the other hand, you may acknowledge that you have a return contract in this lifetime and choose to honor that Soul agreement in a future life.

More specific information on this subject is in my book ***Animal Reincarnation Everything you want to Know***.

If you've never heard about reincarnation as a concept at least give it a try, why not?

In the following pages, there is a Prayer that you can ask your living Pet if it's going to return.

How to ask your pet if it's going to come back

Be sure to ask your question with NO expectations or human emotional filters. Why? Personal hope or wishes will interfere with the answer you receive.

To ask your living pet if it's going to reincarnate, hold its front paws with your hands or place your

hand on the pet's body near its heart, look into its
eyes if possible and ask within your heart or out loud.

**I ask and it is my intent to know if _name_ and I
will be together again in this lifetime. Will _____
return to live with me again in this lifetime?**

Ask 3 times, your heart will hear the answer.

Oftentimes personal emotional upheaval will create an answer or response that you feel is unclear and not factual. To recheck your answers, Use the prayers in a later section, to get a response after your pet is gone.

My guinea pig "Lettuce" is quite a sassy Soul! He needed only one lifetime to make quite an impact upon my heart!

What can affect me receiving Communication, Signs & Visitations?

When "tuned into" or correctly connected with your pet's frequency, one can talk to a pet's energy before, during and throughout the entire transition process while they are going to and living at the Other Side! There is NO waiting or healing time needed. Your pet is OK, alive and well in Spirit the **moment** they exit their pet suit!

There is also NO waiting period to communicate or receive a Sign or Visitation even during their transition process. I watch Pets talk and send Signs even while they were crossing the death line in order to comfort their pet parent's grief! If you don't get a Sign or Visitation for a period of time, don't be upset. Relax, trust and keep asking, and NO you won't be bothering them.

Don't let any AC tell you there is <u>any</u> reason that would delay them from receiving communication, connection or Signs from your pet. If you are told that information, then the reader is unable to access their frequency or to retrieve the information and or is just covering their lack of ability.

If a Communicator/ Psychic has a weak or incorrect connection with your pet's specific frequency, then circumstances and conditions surrounding your pet's death may affect that Reader's ability to connect with your animal's mental energy transmissions, called telepathic impressions.

Some AC's will state that "very ill animals may have a weak "signal" and "animals involved in sudden death trauma, may take a while to communicate" because "they are still in shock from being on the other side" or "healing" or "resting" **(NOT true)**

What determines the quality of the information I receive? It's the Reader's **ability** to access and connect with your pet's varying frequency ranges <u>during any and all events and environments</u>.

Clarity and correct, **very specific** detailed information is all about a precise **accurate** connection. **all** information and **details** that you want to know are available **all the time.**

Why do I mention this? I don't want individuals suffering pet loss to have their hearts hurt even further by receiving incorrect information.

What other things can affect Connection?

It's possible the AC neglected to ask permission to talk with the pet and is not getting 100% cooperation. Animals can also provide untruthful information just like humans. Uncooperative animals might not want to "share." I dealt with a cat that took 2 weeks to get his permission to have a conversation with me! As his health declined he became more agreeable. During 20 years, only one Bichon said "I'm not talking to anyone!" We had to cancel the Reading.

You or your Communicator's **limiting mindsets** affect a Reading. Your disbeliefs will also affect the interpretation and frequency of Signs, messages and

Visitations you receive.

Personal emotional and/or mental filters alter the formation of correct facts in a Reading. Doubting that it's really a communication or connection diminishes your pet's eagerness to keep sending them.

Expectations placed on a Reading can greatly distort the information shared and the reception of accurate knowledge.

Positive expectations about receiving Signs and Visits create a welcoming atmosphere that encourages your pet to send more and more on a continuous basis.

***There is NO time limit on when you can start to receive communication during or after the time a pet crosses over and those Signs can continue for the rest of your life!

Be careful about "free Readings" no matter how desperate you are to connect or have someone tell you it's a Sign from your pet!
YOUR heart will know with NO help!

Remember- Death is always a New Beginning
for a Higher Purpose!

If a newbie pet psychic is practicing and tells you, then that's fair for you to understand that everything might not be correct or accurate.

The "Free Reading" creates a **lot** of heartache and generates a LOT of misinformation if you are hanging on every word. Be careful!

If an AC or Psychic offers an upfront 10 minutes "free reading," you might consider why their business needs to offer discounts and specials.

For over 20 years I have been pioneering the awareness of pet life after death and animal reincarnation to the public.

Finally, people are jumping on the "after death and reincarnation bandwagon." A lot of hearts are hurt, when uneducated individuals tout themselves as being able to access the information YOU want to know or claim that YOUR pet is coming back when in fact it is or has not! The misinformation swirling around about after earth connections and the reincarnation process is mind blowing.

That's why I started my Global Facebook Group for those who want FACTS about life after death processes and who want to learn how to get connections - not hype, sensationalism, drama or "warm and fuzzy" untruths.

It saddens me to hear AC's, psychics or intuitives get some facts correct but still use "believable filler" to mimic knowledgeable about incorrect details. In time, your heart will know what isn't correct.

ALL –every specific detail about your pet's past, present and future life is available in its energy field at <u>all times</u> IF the reader can access it.

KNOW! Somewhere in time we will meet again!

If you get a reincarnation Reading almost every single one of the details below should be covered. Otherwise the reader is not connected or able to access the necessary frequencies.

*Time frame of their return plus where, when and how

*Specifics about what the new pet will look like in its future body, plus very detailed notable markings, colorations and characteristics.

*Checking to see if the Soul's energy matches the exact energy pattern of the first pet. If so I'll tell you it's a "Comeback Kid."

*Explanation of your soul contract which is why your

pet is reincarnating and what his purpose is in your life.

If not reincarnating, you should be told WHY.
I explain the "why" so the client understands the reason for the death and the purpose it serves in their life and new life direction.

Is contacting my pet and asking for Signs & Visits all the time selfish?

As each other's "true love," asking for Signs, Visits or to communicate to stay in touch is not an invasion of privacy. You should ask permission to tap into your pet's energy each time you want to access it for a communication or connection. Your pet may choose to honor your request or they can say "not now, later"

Connection is your pet's decision as to when, where and how to honor your request. Don't be discouraged if you don't get an immediate response in the timeframe or manner you asked.

BE VERY SPECIFIC about your request. (See page 65 for the verbiage requesting Signs).

Also, monitor your emotional level to determine if excessive sadness and sorrow or feeling guilty could be blocking anything.

Grief

If you are reading this book immediately after the passing of your pet, don't get so angry or frustrated that you can't hear what you want to know, get the exact Signs you want or have trouble with the various techniques connecting with your pet.

Although grief and anger are part of the emotional process, **extreme or unnaturally prolonged grief** or

anger will interfere with your ability to connect with or receive Signs from your pet. Have no expectations for the initial outcome. **Your pet is in control!**

Once your emotions are less intense, revisit these techniques and **you will be able** to do them with a little practice.

It takes about 2 weeks to regularly connect with the Other Side "on demand." This does NOT mean that you have to wait that long.

Since your beloved companion is so interwoven into the fabric of your being, **chronic sobbing pushes away your pet's energy. Crying** pulsates in a vibrational direction that pushes away from your body)))))))))))))) It creates a barrier **and hampers their ability to connect to you in the best way possible**! It does not create a welcoming- "come on in" door for **incoming** Signs and signals.

Also, give your "baby" permission to do "as they so choose" when trying to connect with them. Although this is hard to do in critical times, it's about mutual love and respect.

I feel guilt over the circumstances surrounding the death of my pet. Will this affect receiving Signs or Visits?

Yes. Feeling guilt is unnecessary! Circumstances were exactly as they should be for the highest good of all. Guilt energy encapsulates your love in a shell and creates a barrier for reception of their energy.

Again, no matter what happened surrounding the transition of your pet, everything was exactly as both of you planned for that particular time and exit point!!! You made the right decisions, you did not give up on your pet, everything was pre-scripted and there was nothing that should, could or would have been changed for the learning opportunities each of your souls chose to experience.

Please Read that all again!!!

Pet Memorials can prevent Connections

Concentrating your attention, emotions and activities on the **death** of your pet will slow down and repel your pet's connection, Signs and even the re-entry process!

Some people create memorials, grave sites or altars with candles, flowers, photos and keepsake momentos. Others freeze dry or have a taxidermist preserve their pet. Many folks have their animal's ashes incorporated into artwork or made into a bracelet, crystal or another remembrance object.

Ultimately the pet parent goes **to that specific memorialization** and mentally predetermines a connection with their pet thru that "memorial" form. WRONG-

It focuses on their fur suit's "deadness."

Your attitude about them having a connection with you ONLY at a specific memorial's location or object will limit Signs, Visitations and connection.

***A Pet's Spirit and their Love is with you 24/7, ALL the TIME, EVERYWHERE!

Rainbow Bridge Memorabilia

The Rainbow Bridge poem written in the 1980s created an imaginary "place" for dead pets. It's NOT real! Rainbow Bridge named web sites provide pet loss grief support forums and message boards. These online **businesses** encourage posting "dead pet" stuff and ceremonies. Many individuals think they're honoring their pet by paying for products like a photo tribute, buying imaginary flowers or paying for a "residence" in a make-believe place. Heaven is FREE!!!!! How can these memorials be therapeutic remembrances when you have to die to join them? Look at the time you could be spending together while you're still alive!

People need to be aware that a memorial is a reminder of death! It can potentially focus their mind only on the "death," like Fluffy is dead and I have to die to be with him! WRONG! Some believe that deceased pets come and go as they please; others believe a memorial has no influence on the pet's energy on the Other Side. Also, Wrong!

Contrary to the popularity of "memorials," they're also a reminder of what a pet USED to be! The common grievance practice of placing your pet's earth suit in a photo at the Rainbow Bridge sprouting wings, halos and floating on clouds is detrimental to your pet's **living** energy. Why?

He is happy and content,

EXCEPT for one thing.....

IF you've think your pet is ONLY at the make-believe Rainbow Bridge, then your pet will honor your choice and not interrelate with you as a living Pet Spirit

If you've placed their photo in a memorial product claiming "I'll be waiting for you," then <u>YOUR mindset</u> is creating the dead end that your pet is never returning, is not living energy, and much less a Pet Spirit that can and does want to interact with you NOW!!!

These types of memorials also infer you have to die before you're reunited. **NOT so!** IF you believe that fact then your pet will honor your choice and not send Signs nor try to connect with you, much less Visit. FYI You're wasting time you could be enjoying together!

Read this again---Rainbow Bridge is a pretend place created by a Poem. **Pet Heaven** is just a quick after transition electromagnetic adjustment to be on the way back to you (whether in Spirit or Earth form), and **NOT** a permanent destination to stay.

A pet's Soul is alive, well and LIVING Energy **immediately after Transition** and can be everywhere at any time!

In order to be a positive participant after the loss of a pet, choose to:

* Celebrate your ongoing LIVING Soul bond and new Spirit journey together.

* acknowledge and continue your pet's never-ending love!

* be open minded to the possibility of a pet's return.

Visit their "Celebration" spot with excitement, and knowledge that together you're continuing on a new journey. That's "GOOD grief!!!"

Pet Loss Beliefs

1. Rainbow Bridge
   * Your Pet dies and waits for you at a make believe place created by a Poem called Rainbow Bridge
   * You have to die to be with your Pet again

2. Pet Afterlife & Animal Life After Death
   * Your Pet discards it's "fur suit" & transitions to Heaven.
   * He/ she instantly becomes a happy, healthy & healed
   * eternal Living Energy called a Pet Soul or Spirit
   * who sends you Signs and
   * Visits with you to continue being a part of your life &
   * to continue your Never Ending Love together!

How to Create an Environment to receive Signs

When Animals on the Other Side take the time to expend their energy to choose to be around to connect, comfort and communicate with you, enjoy each experience.

Death can NOT separate us
I'm ALWAYS
with YOU!!

Oftentimes people second guess and over analyze their visitations and Signs, "Was that really my Pet?" Don't doubt or question their ability to send and your ability to receive these after death connections and communications. Be thrilled! What a Gift!

NO, you are not crazy!!! You are aware of "all there is!"

*Trust. Don't doubt or question your Pet's ability to send and your heart's ability to recognize after death connections and communications.

*Usually Signs come when you are relaxed with no expectations. Try to make a quiet time each day, and ask your Pet to contact you then.

*You may want to visualize scenarios with your pet. Some people find that is a good way for them to relate. Personally, I prefer the Specific prayers, so there is NO confusion about what I am asking and when I'd like to have as a response.

*Talk with your Pet out loud or in your heart as if he's right there, because usually she is! Accepting, praising and interacting with their Spirit creates unlimited access and receptivity to your pet's connection and communication from the Other Side!

*Other people praying for you to have a connection with your Pet doesn't work!
YOU have the heart connection. Your beloved companion is part of the fiber of **your** being.
YOU can do this all by yourself!

* Choose a **Positive** support group that encourages you to seek answers and move forward.

* No matter what Species your beloved companion is, they CAN connect with you.

I loved "Fishy" and was **heartbroken** when he transitioned! He kept an eye on me and followed me as best he could. I spent endless hours talking with and watching him swim. It was calming... He "got me through" some very tough life learning opportunities   May he be blessed!

Pet Spirits know
Death is not final
or the end of their Road
It's the beginning of a new life
as Living Energy.

Live, love, laugh & share with Them
now, forevermore and always!

How to Connect with your Pets

Guardian Angels can come in Fur!

Animal Communication sessions are a great way to connect with your pet and can contribute information for your peace of mind. However, ask yourself the questions below:

*Are you being obsessive about contacting and

receiving Signs from your pet because you feel you can't move on?

*Are you SO upset and consumed by sorrow for the vacated Pet suit that you are unrealistically lonely?

*Are you so co-dependent on your relationship that you can't let go and allow your Soul to evolve with the lessons you learned and shared?

There is a time to seek awareness and a time to move forward. *Please go to bereavement counseling if necessary.* Emotional "I can't get over this" attitudes and I want to "be with my pet" are unhealthy for you and your animal's spiritual energy.

When an animal's Earth Job is complete, that segment of their Soul contract is also complete with you. If anyone tells you "your pet is staying around because you need them to" or "not crossing over" or "not moving on" just because you miss them so much or because you want them to, **WRONG!** A pet sends Signs and Visits from the Other Side because they want to comfort and connect with you through the Love and joy you shared, NOT for a negative needy reason. You need to move forward too.

An "I can't let go- dead end" attitude dishonors all the joy and love your pet unconditionally shared with you. **Your Pet wants you to be happy**! That's why they are in your life in the first place. Just because they vacated their fur suit does NOT stop them from sharing joy and happiness with you in Spirit form.

It's **your Earth attitude** that can celebrate what you now HAVE or cause the relationship memory to be a septic tank of sadness!

Choose to celebrate their Spirit being alive and well. Don't focus on the discarded Earth Suit. You're moving into another wonderful chapter of sharing unless YOU choose not to allow it!

Think about it, without a fur suit and "time", your Pet's Spirit can be with you anywhere, anytime, any way in a nano second! That's 24/7/365 unrestricted unconditional sharing and loving!

For the 30 to 40% of pet parents that will experience a "Comeback Kid," there will be a time when your pet will no longer respond to your requests because he has moved into reformulating to come back or readapting to being on Earth. However, **don't** automatically think it's a huge signal that they will reincarnate.

Your Pet's Spirit might not respond to requests because he doesn't feel the necessity to do so or is operating on HIS timing. They are in charge!
For example, after Mike's transition, he stayed with me during those early years. Afterwards his visits

became less frequent. Mike recognized I had grown beyond requiring his presence to move forward in life. 20+ years later he's still and ALWAYS with me for special occasions, emotional support/opinions/ decisions or protection.

Now, let's learn how YOU can connect directly your Pet.
MOST IMPORTANT ***Before you begin any contact with the Other Side, be sure to protect yourself! Why?

When you open a connection to the Other Side, you **only** want your pet to respond. You need to be **very specific** so you won't be a portal for any and all energies and entities that want to communicate and connect with someone else on Earth.

Protecting yourself requires getting your prayers and intent on a defined tract. Learn how to Pray in order to carefully craft and direct your requests.

How to Pray: Be SPECIFIC!

Pet Spirits live in "forever time" and your Earth suit/body lives in finite time, so you need to be very specific about what you on Earth want from those on the Other Side. Say:

I ASK: "ask and ye shall receive." It's a Universal Law that all those in charge of your soul's contract must respond. You're asking all those in charge of your soul to help you, now! Why not use ALL the powers you have on heaven and earth that are available to you???

It is MY INTENT (with a "T" **NOT** Inten**d with a D**) that brings your prayers into the NOW, in this incarnation, at this very moment in time.
YOU MUST BE SPECIFIC!!!!!!!!!!!!!!!

Animals in Heaven live in "forever" time so be VERY specific about exactly what you want and in the VERY SPECIFIC timeframe of what you want. Not being specific (intend) is never never land, or "which incarnation?" etc. to those on the Other Side.

I suggest that you say your prayer 3 times. 3 is the universal number.
*The first time sets your free will to ask for help,
*the second time your prayer creates intent
*the third time to me, means you're really focused on getting this accomplished!

Use the words **Now, Forevermore and Always**.

"Now," brings your prayer into the now, i.e. the present. Your Pets on the Other Side operate in a timeless "forever" and for Them to respond to your command you must state "now", otherwise your Guides and Pets will be asking "in which incarnation, past life or parallel life do you want this done?"

"Forevermore," takes the prayer into all energy realms, incarnations and time frames. "Always," makes the prayer request continuous with no lapses.

At the finale of your request **Say: So be it, it is done**. Thank you. "So be it," brings the prayer into your present situation. "It is done," makes the prayer a reality, NOW!

First, it's best (although not necessary) to take off your shoes and say your Protection Prayer

****

Protection Prayer:
I ask and it is my intent, to surround myself in a seamless mirrored--(bubble or cocoon) of the Christ White Light (or whomever is your Higher Power), to protect me now, forevermore and always. Only allow the energy or entities which are for my soul's highest and best good to come thru. So be it, it is done. Thank you.

This is THE PRAYER to say at any time in any place, whenever you want to protect yourself from any and all energies and entities.

Why do I use the words seamless and mirrored?
Seamless means nothing comes in or out of your being or environment unless you allow it. The concept of mirrored means that any negative energy or entity, event or whatever that is aimed at you, reflects back to the sender so that you will not be drained or affected. SO, easy!

*** If you change the wording of a prayer you will receive different results. ***

Our radio show on "Animal Communication gone Wrong" on Pet Life Radio.com was done because this is important information!

Next, ask your Pet's permission to contact and work with them either outloud or telepathically with your mind or heart. You will hear the answer in your inner consciousness.

NOW You are ready to request your Pet's Spirit to send Signs, come to visit, contact or energetically connect with you.

REMEMBER ** A major mistake that causes disconnection and all sorts of problems-is- **Do NOT use IntenD** use **INTENT!**
Protect yourself first. (page 80)
BEFORE you start each Prayer or Request.

****

How to Ask Your Pet for Signs say:
I ask and it is my intent to contact my pet previously called _____. I ask _____ to send me a Sign that I can easily recognize and understand within the next hour or _____ days to tell me what he wants me to know. So be it it is done, Thank you _ (Fluffy) _

****

How to Ask Your Pet to Visit in Dreams:
I ask and it is my intent to contact my pet previously called _____.
I ask _____ to visit me in my dreams tonight or during my nap or_____. I ask _____ to show me what he wants me to know in a way that I can easily understand and will remember. So be it, it is done, Thank you!

FYI- Practice about 30 minutes a day or whatever feels comfortable for you. It works!

If you want your pet to answer questions in your dreams, be **VERY specific** about what you are requesting.

To Ask a Specific Question in a Dream:

I ask and it is my intent to contact my pet previously called _____. I ask _____to visit me in my dreams tonight or during my nap or_____. (Timeframe like within 48 hours) I ask _____ to show and or tell me the answer to the following question in a way that I can easily understand and will remember. <u>Fluffy</u>, Why do you_____or Are you made at me or _____. So be it, it is done, Thank you! (Use Pet's name then Ask ONLY one SINGLE SPECIFIC question)

I kept a notebook of Mike's answers. When I was feeling sad or lonely I'd go back and revisit his messages to me.

You might want to keep a journal of answers, dreams and visits. Many years later it will STILL be an educational and interesting read!

Oftentimes a person will say prayers for a period of time and have no results. Sometimes it's not the correct timing for you to know that answer. Otherwise, if no answer is the case, ask again! Usually the "askor" did not use SPECIFIC verbiage and "changed up" or threw in a "few of my own words." Additionally, your grief may be so strong that it's interfering with receiving Signs. Trust your pet's Spirit will answer you. **Doubting prevents them from completing your requests.**

How soon after my pet's death can I use the techniques below? Immediately is fine! There are no time constraints for contacting a deceased pet.

How to Sense / Recognize / Identify a Pet's Energy presence (YouTube video 20)

I ask and it is my intent to contact my Pet
_____, so I can feel _____ here NOW.
I ask _____ to put your paw (nose, head, whatever) into my _____hand   NOW.
So be it. It is done. Thank you.

****** Use the hand that you do NOT write with, that's your "receiving energy" hand.

Brent Atwater's
Just Plain Love® Books presents

If you're uncomfortable feeling/ sensing/ recognizing their energetic presence, use the prayer for asking to see him in my dreams on page 82.

Always use the Protection prayer on page 80 first.
I say this prayer 3 times to create intent, focus and clarity. Use these **exact** words. These words protect you from having unwanted energies or entities visit.

IF you are extremely emotional at this point in time you might not be able to sense/ feel / recognize their Spirit's energy. Take the time to calm down! This method works! My Mother's 86-year-old Garden Club members were able to do this.

You will begin to recognize/ identify their energy when you feel tingles or pulsating in your hand, or "thick weighty" air, a sense of pressure or cold or maybe a warm air area that is different from the surrounding air, or like pressing on a balloon. NO, you are NOT crazy, this is real!! You have now felt and identified YOUR pet's specific and individual energy pattern.

If it doesn't work at first, try again. If it works the first time and then not again, ask YOURSELF what are YOU doing to block the exchange of energy.

If you did it once you can always do it again!

Once you've identified their specific individual energy pattern, it is always available!" Sometimes it takes up to 2 weeks before your pet will show up "on demand" because their energy resides in Eternity i.e. no time clock. Various research materials suggest that you "contact" Spirits (pets and people too!) at the same time each day for quicker results.

*** I suggest you practice these techniques about 30 minutes each day for at least 2 weeks until your pet responds on a regular basis and then move to the next technique.

Can I do these techniques with any Pet that I lost years ago? Yes! Every pet has a unique energy pattern that you can learn to identify when you ask that specific pet to show up. Kim shared "At the one-year anniversary of Chippers' transition I was really struggling. I asked him to place his paw in my hand and sure enough, IMMEDIATELY I felt the tingles in my hand! He curled up and lay down next to me until I went to sleep, just like he always used to do. I could feel him lying there next to me, with his head on my arm. It brought me a great deal of peace just knowing that he's still here when I need him!!!"

Now that my pet's Spirit is visiting me, what do I do? Enjoy your new awareness and your pet's Living Spirit. Teach him tricks -After death connection is very real!

It's best to invite only one pet at a time to visit so you won't open an entrance way for other unwanted energies to slip through.

If I contact my animal's Spirit, am I interrupting him from whatever he is supposed to be doing on the Other Side?
NO! Why would he be busy with anything else? His connection is with you! However, being impatient can and will delay your request's response. It's your Pet's choice to respond when they want to do so. Sometimes extreme eagerness to receive instant gratification with an immediate response is an issue stemming from **your** grief.
Trust the timing will be perfect.

FYI- Sometimes your cherished animal companion will just "show up" in a Visitation to "check on you" just to let you know they're OK. Enjoy the Gift!

How to Interact with a Pet's Spirit

Before Mike died, I did not know "interacting with living energy/ Spirit" on the Other Side was even possible! I'd heard about it, but blew it off as "airy Fairy." Plus, being raised as a Christian, I was really afraid to be involved in anything "like that!"

After his Transition and from the Other Side, Mike patiently instructed me on how to do these interactive techniques. After I learned how to recognize his energy (page 83) and then interact with his specific Spirit, (page 88) we would hold hands when I was afraid and he would kiss me every night before I went to sleep. His living energy Spirit slept beside me for months after he had vacated his biological being.

Growing up I always heard that "God is Love." Through my experiences with Mike's after death communication and learning these techniques I totally understand love transcends everything and is everlasting! I KNOW beyond a shadow of a doubt that a Soul's energy and love is forever and always -- alive and well and NEVER ending!

Request for a Spirit to show up "on demand" so you can interact/ play together

I ask and it's my intent for __ Fluffy's_ Spirit to Visit me NOW.

I ask _____ to visit me NOW

I ask _____ to visit me NOW

I ask _ to visit me NOW SO be it it is done.

Thank you _____.

How do I confirm my Pet has "showed up?"
Use the Exercise on page 85 to have them put their paw in your hand.
Once they do that on a regular basis, then use the prayer above and follow the instructions below.

Now that your Pet has "shown up," and you know the feel of their specific energy pattern, let's learn how to connect with their **Spirit** on an ongoing basis.

1. Rub your hands together until they are warm in order to activate the nerve endings in your palms and fingertips so you can sense energy to the "max."
If you need to "refresh" your sensory sensitivity, just do this "warming up" exercise and start over **as many times as necessary.**

2. Spread your fingers apart with about -at least- a half inch of space between each finger, like a wide toothed comb. That increases your sensitivity to feeling energy. Don't do stiff fingers, bend them slightly although spread apart in a relaxed manner.

3. Very SOFTLY, as if you are trying to touch the dust on butterfly wings, start SLOWLY sweeping your hands horizontally back and forth within about a 4-foot-wide path and within a 4-foot-high rectangular area in the vicinity you sense your pet is located.

Continuously scan for their energy back and forth left to right or vice versa and top to bottom through your designated space. Keep working in rectangular quadrants until you feel and or sense "something" in the manner that YOUR body registers/ receives energy input.

Your pet will or can feel like: a thicker, puffier, denser, usually cooler area or a section that causes your hand to tingle. It can also feel like "fat air," a warm balloon or like two magnets pushing against your hands. That's your Pet's Spirit! Your heart will KNOW it's them!

*** The softer and more consistent your movements are and the slower (i.e. don't rush this) you approach any energy field, the greater the sensory input you receive.

Don't be so fearful or doubtful that you brush off reality!

Being "sensitive to a different feel of air space" is how you progress. When you get really good at this, you can learn to feel the edges of their Heavenly form. If you get REALLY good, you can feel them walking on your pillow or getting in your lap or sleeping beside you.

Be patient and practice, practice, practice! This will allow your tactile recognition of various and specific

Spirits to occur more rapidly.

Don't get frustrated, in time, this works.

Now, you and your Pet's Spirit can play together for the rest of your life on Earth to continue your never-ending love story!

However- If your animal is regrouping to reincarnate, his energy field will be thinner and more difficult to detect as time grows closer for his return.

What's the importance of this exercise?
Once you have learned to identify, connect and interact with your Pet's specific energy pattern, then you will be more "in tune" when they Visit.
***** Not everyone can do all of these exercises.
We each have different abilities for each lifetime.**

Can these techniques be used to contact and connect with People on the Other Side? Yes

My YouTube show has Videos demonstrating these techniques. Subscribe so you won't miss anything.

How to See a Pet's Spirit

When you look at a Pet Spirit, it will appear like a "see through" steam, cloudy or sparkly, translucent version of what their form looked like on earth. Usually a pet will appear in their healthy mid-life physical form. Some people will be able to do this exercise others won't have this ability in this lifetime.

Step 1: Ask your deceased pet's energy to show up. **I ask and it is my intent to contact the energy previously known as _____, so that I can feel him here NOW.**

Step 2: Once your deceased pet has responded and you have located and can recognize their energy presence with you, then state:

Prayer to See a Pet Spirit
I ask and it is my intent to see my deceased _pet name_ Spirit form now, I ask and it is my intent to see my deceased __pet name ___Spirit form now, I ask and it is my intent to see my deceased ___pet's name__) Spirit form now.

2. Then close your eyes tight and say **"shift energy and refocus now."**

3. Open your eyes softly, try not to blink. Call you pet by saying

_____ show yourself to me, in front of me NOW, show yourself to me, in front of me now, show yourself to me, in front of me now.

If you have this skill set, in time they will show up!!! Be patient. It may take 2 weeks or more but they will show up! If you have glanced them out of the corner of your eye, now ask them to "**show up in front of me**," so you will have a very clear vision of them!

Talk out loud and encourage them to help you make a better connection to communicate with them! Remember you were a team on Earth, now you are a team across the Veils.

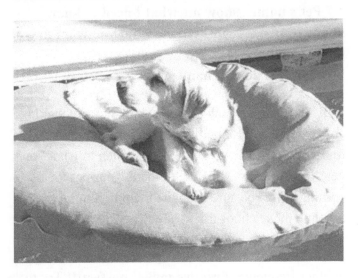

Do you want more information?
When your pet has taken the time to reformulate for you to see them, whether out of the corner of your eye or across the room, it's an opportune time to ask for more information.

I often saw Possum Kitty running from room to room and Hairy Kitty's Spirit sleeping in my open office drawer. Sometimes I see my yellow lab "Boo Bear" running across the golf course with his ball, to show me he's happy.

Prayer for More Information Say:
"__Pet's name_ show me what I need to know about you now." Or "tell me what you want me to know now"
So be it, it is done, Thank you

YOU can also say this request while they are making any appearance. Remember repeating each phrase 3 times makes it REAL clear! Then listen to what you hear in your heart. Be sure to thank your pet for coming. Also, be sure to invite them to return anytime those choose!

It will take a while for you to get used to accessing another frequency **Practice makes perfect!!!** Try to practice when you can focus and not be distracted.

Some people will be able to do all techniques others only a few depending upon their energy sensitivity. Either way, your Pet is waiting to connect with you! Energetic connection and pet communication are DIFFERENT.
You CAN CONNECT with your Pet!

Pet Spirits
want you to know
Sometimes we are
Angels &
Spirit Guides
in Earth suits
Loving &
Watching
over you.
After transition,
we watch over, guide
& LOVE you
Forever & Always!

After Death Signs from Pet Afterlife
& Animals in Heaven Book by Brent Atwater

Brent Atwater's
Just Plain Love® Books presents

Signs from the Other Side-
Your Pet's Never-Ending Love Story!

First and foremost-   NO, you are NOT "crazy."

Can asking for Signs immediately after Transition stop our fur babies crossing over or being OK? NO.

The minute a pet vacates its earth suit their energy becomes Spirit. NO amount of asking or anything else can affect a pet from crossing over.

The only possible exception is one pet I watched going through transition at the veterinarian's office. It had to make 2 attempts to separate and vacate from its **very tight**-fitting earth suit. (YouTube Video 34) That's the ONLY time in 20 years I've seen anything slow down a transition over the death line.

Pet's signs will be very clear and distinct. Your heart WILL recognize and KNOW it's them! If you wonder "is that Fluffy?" Or think "it might be," it most likely IS!!

Animals in Heaven always send the most appropriate Sign that will touch your heart to heal your grief in the most perfect way and timing. **There are NO coincidences**. NEVER doubt their ability, persistence or creativity!

NO, you are NOT "crazy."

How Pets decide what Signs to Send

Think about it. Pets don't know when you are going to ask for a Sign. They have to consider and coordinate a lot of factors. They need to determine where you are and when, how they will send THE Sign that will mean the most to you. And wonder if you will listen to their subliminal suggestions to see, feel, hear or experience that Sign.
TRUST your pet's creative choice and timing.

I want to thank each member of my global Facebook Pet family, my Facebook Page followers, and my

YouTube, Instagram, Periscope and Twitter fans who allowed me to share their life's experiences and images of their Pet's Signs and visitations from the Other Side as examples for our readers to know you can't make this stuff up!

Animals in Heaven are VERY innovative and persistent in unimaginable, to the max ways!

We invite you to join my Facebook page and Group to share your experiences and ask questions during my LIVE streaming Q & A Events.

ANIMALS & PETS

Can Animals send Signs through other Pets? Yes.

Do animals on the Other Side direct the behavior of pets on Earth? Yes.

It's a process called "Over souling."

How can you tell if it's an Over Soul arrangement with a deceased Pet? The living Pet is "acting like" the old pet. Key word "acting like"

Brent Atwater's
Just Plain Love® Books presents

"Over Soul" Agreements

He has NEVER stopped loving you..

When Animals are in Spirit, in some incidences it's more difficult for them to communicate with us in certain ways. Example your extreme grief, guilt or anger is blocking their direct Signs. In order to bypass that hurdle, animals often use indirect ways to contact you. That is why a pet may use the Oversouling process.

Many pet parents are so distraught over the death of their dog, cat, horse, finned, shelled or feathered beloved companion that they want to believe their living pet has become the deceased pet. This is a common error created by grief's hopeful and wishful expectations.

Over Souling is when the deceased pet in Heaven directs and guides the living animal on "what to do" and "how to behave." That's the "over soul" agreement in action. It's a contract made between the deceased pet and the living animal.

A pet being "over souled" makes you think "**he acts like my old pet**" by displaying recognizable and very identifiable characteristics. However, an "over souled" pet does not ignite that deep and certain knowing that "this IS my reincarnated pet" on an ongoing basis.

With an over souled pet, you will inwardly question yourself and have some doubts. Your misgiving and disbelief is a very informative real answer for your heart.

***Over souling is an intermittent process, NOT a permanent arrangement, although it can be an off and on agreement for years

In over souling, the deceased pet's energy does NOT enter the living animal, **it only visits**. If the Spirit energy did permanently merge with the living pet that process would be a "Walk-in" or Soul braid. Both are one of 3 ways to reincarnate.
(See my book **Animal Reincarnation**)

Merging with and into a living pet's energy on an intermittent come and go basis would make the living animal very sick. Why? Because each visit or merge into the living pet's body would disrupt and alter the electromagnetics of the earth pet's life energy. Accommodating the coming and goings would make the living pet very sick or likely to have seizures. Therefore, **over souling is done by directives and NOT mini merges.**

The over souling process is also a way your pet can just check in to keep in touch with you, let you know they are OK and are there for you in Spirit, in addition to seeing that everything is going the way "it should be" according to their Heavenly perspective.

If you miss and want your pet back so badly, wishful thinking on your part may create difficulty and confusion in telling whether it's a straight reincarnation or an "Over soul" process. However, no matter how often or how long the Over souling occurs, the pet parent WILL eventually determine what's going on and know it's not a permanent "Come Back" kid.

Will there be a time that my deceased pet stops coming around? NO, only if you tell them to go away! Pets can send signs for the rest of YOUR earth life!

From the Netherlands, Imke wrote "After our conversation the neighbor's cat stayed with us for 3 weeks because her human family was on holiday. She acted like Puma. She would put her paw in my cup of water and sat on the corner of the table while I was on my laptop just like Puma did. Obviously, Puma was directing her, how would this strange cat know what to do! It was such a nice experience when I recognized that Puma was over souling her!"

Below is an example of how energy is energy no matter what form it is comes in; Bun Bun the Bunny over souled a cat to get his message across.

Brenda "About a month ago, I found Gary this tabby cat on the street and immediately knew I was taking him home. Fast forward to tonight. I am in the bathtub soaking my grief away when Gary comes right up to the tub, puts his paws on the edge and looks at me just like my bunny has done so many times. Wow I have to ask are you Bun Bun? The very next second Gary jumps up on the edge of the tub and stares at me. I quickly grabbed my phone to take a few pictures. Gary also follows me around the house ever where just like my bunny did. I am still learning about Oversouling, but I like it as a Sign!"

Carol wrote "Tiny, my dachshund, was with me for 10 years. I had him at 26 days old so I needed to bottle feed him for a while. He slept by my side at night for the entire 10 years! I even brought him daily to the office. When he passed away, I did not want to have a pet anymore. I was depressed and cried all the time. However, 2 months after, I could hear the voice in my mind saying I should look at the internet for pups on sale. I was hesitant, but finally gave in. I saw a posting of some dach puppies for sale but it was the dad who was in the picture, not the pups. So, I went to the place to see the pups. One pup immediately ran to me. I knew I would buy him. After two weeks, I went to get "Frankie". When we got home, he ran to where Tiny used to sleep. There was nothing there, no pillows anymore, yet Frankie just cuddled himself comfortably and slept soundly. When he woke up, we stared at each other's eyes. I felt something so I cried and said, are you Tiny? Did you come back? If you are, come kiss me. Frankie ran to me and tried to reach my face. I bowed down. Suddenly, he licked my tears trying to dry them up like Tiny use to do. There were so many more instances that proved these two dachsies that I loved so much are working together to keep me happy!"

From Australia Theresa texted "Dru acting like Baxter (lying in B's favourite spot and thumping her tail just like him), reached up to scratch my nose just like Baxter did the first time I met him. This was our "secret signal" that I told him to do when he returns. It's important to note this behavior is TOTALLY out of character for Dru. I know Baxter was Oversouling him!"

Michele "Is it possible for my cat Princess to somehow act like my cat Jazzy? Princess has been playing, the hide and seek game and other silly things like Jazzy did. Is this Princess?

A: Yes.

When a living pet displays the old pet's behavior it is Oversouling.

Ashley- "Would it be possible for an animal you lost to come back to you in another animal?   A few weeks ago, Riley started acting really strange. His eyes turned the same color as Hailey's and he was doing things he has never done before. When Dustin and I had Hailey, she used to lay in between us every single night for attention. We called it the cuddle zone.

One night Riley came up on the bed with Hailey's eyes and came in between us acting just like Hailey. I said her name Hailey and she responded. It wasn't long before she was gone. But does that really happen or am I just crazy?"

A: That is an example of oversouling and an over imaging visitation in the eyes so you would KNOW for sure who the Visitation was from. Good Girl Hailey!"

Over Imaging (see page 242) is like Oversouling, but is usually found in Reincarnated Pets. It's a visitation process the old pet uses to insure the parent understands the new body is housing the old Soul.

Animals in Nature as Signs

In his book **Animal-Speak** (one of my favorite resource books about nature animals' spiritual purpose and meaning in your life), Ted Andrews believes that seeing Signs embodied as animals in nature, can add new layers to our awareness. These occurrences, coupled with animal imagery and other nature totems, can be an extended way of learning about ourselves interfacing with and being educated by "the invisible world" of "all there is."

Additionally, ongoing Signs that you clearly identify, can in time, become a signal to rethink what we are doing and to reexamine how we are interpreting the world around us. Animal and nature Signs can be reminders of universal wisdom, or nudgies to "consider this thought," or a "heads up" about what's coming in the future. Usually, through a specific Sign, the Universe is illuminating a concept for you to think about or a reminder to look at ALL possibilities or a precise directive for you to consider. For example, when I see Hummingbirds and Dragonflies, I know my life is going to have changes coming in the future.

Directing another Animal to say Hello

Sometimes a pet in Heaven will ask another animal to let you know they are thinking about you. It's not Oversouling because it's a one-time singular event. It's like asking a friend to tell that another friend that you were thinking about them.

Here's an example of a Pet using a Frog to say hello.

"After Nikki transitioned, the following night while I was grieving, I went outside and was standing there mourning her, when I saw a frog on the other side of the street hopping down the street toward me. When it got directly across from me, it stopped and turned towards me and just sat there staring at me for about 30 seconds. I stared back and finally ask "Is that you Nikki?" The frog stared a little longer then turned and continued its journey down the street."

That was a big "Hello" and "I'm OK" Sign.
What's important in this scenario is the fact that Renee asked the frog if it was Nikki. By acknowledging that she might have in fact received Nikki's Sign, the frog could move on because it had completed its agreement, and had expanded Renee's awareness of how Signs can be sent.

FYI "Frog is a Symbol of Transformation. Like the Butterfly, Frog symbolism represents transformation on many levels. Frog spirit animal also has many lives, as he begins as a tadpole and slowly transforms into the Frog that can live in two worlds, in the water and on land.

Frog also is a symbol of Spiritual Cleansing and has powers to renew mind, body and spirit. Obviously, Nikki's Mom Renee's spirit was uplifted knowing she was OK.

Frog additionally represents awakening your

beautiful authentic truth. Nikki, was using the frog to extend the spiritual awareness process of her pet parent whose Heart immediately responded to their Soul's connection.

Bird Spirits want you to know "I'm always with you when you feel alone! You're NEVER alone!"

After Death Signs from Pet Afterlife & Animals in Heaven
Book by Brent Atwater

BIRDS

"The day after my dog Winnie transitioned there were a few Cardinals in my tree in the front yard – I've noticed them every day since. After my Reading with Brent, a cardinal came right up to the window when I opened the blinds fluttering its wings and went back to the tree as if it was Winnie saying hello. Even when I take walks, Cardinals often appear and follow Jessie and me even across streets."

FYI the Cardinal's presence in our life reflects a time to renew our vitality. Seeing a Cardinal suggests we look at developing and accepting a new look at ourselves and our own self-esteem and what we have to offer others. As a totem, Cardinals reflect an inner desire to embrace the feminine aspects of intuition and to understand the role of giving and receiving. Cardinal is a reminder that at any time of the year, there are always new opportunities to embrace our own importance and vitality in our own roles in life.

Julie's deceased dog Sam told her he wanted to fly free. This is what occurred: "After my dream, the day was just breaking, when I was awakened by loud tapping noises. At my window was a **Crow** flapping its wings and tapping loudly at the window pane. He continued to do do for a while, then flew away. I thought this was strange and following my dream it might be significant. The next morning, I opened the back door to go feed my birds and there was a racing pigeon, sitting near the step. He was so tame, that I fed him and gave him water. He stayed all day, listening to me talking and going about my day, then flew off at dusk. Today, that Pigeon turned up again and stayed all day once more, almost coming into the house at one point. There was also a blackbird that appeared the same day as Sam's passing, who sat right by me and spread his wings out in the sunshine and bathed, while I poured my heart out to him. He has now become a tame and common visitor. The same evening, my daughter Sarah had a seagull tapping her window too." Sam was very expressive and persistent. Plus, he notified Julie in her dream that he would be coming to Visit in bird form!

FYI Pigeons are part of the dove family and remind you to find strength and stay the course through challenges.

Doves and Mourning Doves are Spirit reminding you to be at Peace, let go of negative thoughts and focus on Love. It's also a message that you're receiving Blessings from Above, or in this case Pet Heaven or Rainbow Bridge.

DUCK & GEESE- Personal Example

People also use animals that are symbolic of your relationship together or that have a special meaning to you. My fiancé Mike loved Geese who mate for life. These Geese were photographed in my yard on the anniversary of the day he died. Also, either the Geese or a Mallard and its mate (who also mate for life) always show up on our Anniversary. I know its Mike letting me know he's thinking of us forever and always!

If you have Ducks or Geese visit you after the loss of a beloved pet, here's the meaning:

"There are eight species of Geese in North America. This is very symbolic in that the number eight is so similar to the symbol for infinity. It reflects an ability to move forward or backward. It reflects movement, and in the case of the Goose, a call to the spiritual quest. Anytime the Goose comes, you can expect to have the imagination stirred toward new travels to distant places -whether in the body or in the mind."

FOXES are usually sent by Pets to watch over you from a distance. Foxes can be a silent guardian from the shadows.

"Fox symbolizes the feminine magic of camouflage and shape-shifting. The Fox is the Protector at the Edge of the Unconscious. Fox lives in the instants between evening and night, between nighttime and dawn, in the auric energies around our bodies, and in the spaces between waking consciousness and deep sleep."

INSECTS

LADYBUGS herald a time of good luck and dreams come true, letting you know that goals are possible. However, Ladybug asks you to be cautious and let things flow at a natural pace and not be rushed. Ladybug also signals you to live in your own truth and knowing.

After Daryl's dog Hunter's death, he sent triple Signs. "First a Ladybug, followed Daryl out into the yard, then he was being buzzed by a hummingbird, and then a butterfly and to top it off...A Squirrel! Hunter's Favorite. I would have to be particularly dense not to get those messages."

Francis shared "the day I put Echo to sleep a Ladybug landed on my Hubby in our car as were driving down the road leaving the vet's office. I also saw a half a rainbow on a sunny day. I know that was a Sign from her letting me know she's ok" Plus "in the last few days, I think all the Ladybugs that are not normally around are from my sweet Echo."

It's important to note that each of these pet parents without question immediately associated the appearance of a Ladybug with their pet. If you feel the Sign is sent by your pet, it probably is.

Pet Death is like a seed.
It's the begining of life
as LIVING Energy
in Spirit form.
Love is Never Ending!

After Death Signs
book by Brent Atwater
© Dianne Virga Photographer

Prayer to ask if a Sign was sent by your Pet
"_Fluffy _   I ask you to tell me NOW, did you
send the <u>Ladybug</u> as a Sign for me today,
Yes or No?

I would ask 3 times. You'll hear the answer in your
heart or mind.

How do I know it's not me answering myself?
Answers from Spirit usually come instantaneously, i.e. the IMMEDIATE response you hear. If you're slow to answer, it's probably your mind doing a quick analysis and answering you.

BOOKS

Oftentimes a book will fall off the shelf and land on the floor to the exact information you need to receive or read. Or a bookmark may lead you to the perfect passage. Even more interesting is when you randomly open a book to the exact subject you're thinking about. All of those occurrences are NOT a coincidence.

Even reading a book can be the catalyst for a sign. Morgana wrote "while reading Brent's book about Pet Loss to learn how to contact my dog, I saw a feather falling down from a tree that captured my attention! I guess she was sending a blessing from Pet Heaven to let me know she wants me to learn more!"

Frankie says "One of Bear's ways of sending me Signs is also to show me his name in print at random times. In the past few weeks, he has shown me his name in many various places almost daily. I will read something that normally I would have ignored and there it is! And pennies everywhere!! Love you and thank you my buddy"

Amanda "The night after Winston died, June 29th in my grief I asked for Winston to give me a sign that he was ok. The first thought that popped into my head was to look in the coffee table, in the middle drawer which faces the TV. I got out of bed and looked in this drawer where I found two books I had forgotten I had. One was about Animals and the Afterlife and the other was all about life after death. I knew it was Winston guiding me to learn about his new perspective."

You got the Butterflies & Feathers
I sent didn't you???
And it was me
who played
our favorite
song!

Animal Reincarnation Animal Life After Death Book by Brent Atwater

BUTTERFLIES are a category all unto itself. They are considered the Universal symbol of reincarnation and rebirth. Why?

It's because their life cycle represents the reincarnation cycle. Think about it, a caterpillar entombs itself in a cocoon and suspends its life for a period of time only to reemerge back on Earth to experience another life as a beautiful butterfly. WOW!

Butterflies may come into your home, sit on your shoulder, fly around your environment or follow you. Many people speak of seeing white butterflies after the death of a beloved companion. **White butterflies are said to be sent from the Angels and made from a portion of their wings.**

Any butterfly is a solid sign that you're getting a message to let you know everything is OK and that a Soul is reborn on the Other Side. And any butterfly symbol such as seen on the side of a truck, a T shirt, on a napkin or in a magazine or a thousand other ways that it could come into your life is a Sign!

Caution- Every butterfly sign is not a guaranteed sign of reincarnation. If your pet is reincarnating, there will be a multitude of different signs reinforcing the same message- not just one from of Sign.

Danika wrote "I saw a white little butterfly flying around the flowers and door to my house. We have never seen the butterflies at all until my baby passed away. Now we've seen them three times. She always met me at the door when I got home from work. I saw the butterfly at the door right after I got home; I really think that was a sign from her."

Maria said "a few weeks after she passed, I was crying in my car regarding lack of connection and begging for one. Within moments a butterfly flew in front of my windshield. I've never noticed butterflies in my neighborhood before. Houses are so close together. I felt this was a sign"

From Australia Leanne wrote "I decided to make a small section of my garden a memorial for my boy - just plant some flowers that he liked to sleep amongst at our old place and get a little bench with some words engraved on it. Anyway, I went out there a few days ago and there were little butterflies everywhere!! JUST in that part of the garden, they flew all around me, I smiled so big!"

Kris "After Chewy passed a good friend gave us an ornament for his grave with a butterfly that is supposed to circle a Sunflower. It has never worked. Upon visiting Chewy's grave in the Spring, we heard this clicking noise and we looked--- that butterfly was flying around the Sunflower. We couldn't believe it was finally working. It was like Chewy was saying I am still here Mom and Dad and I miss you!"

Spirit energy is electromagnetic energy, so it can easily affect the electromagnetics of almost any electronic device-even mechanical butterflies to say it's me!

FYI   Spirit/ "ghost" and Orb energy can be measured on special machines to determine the strength and frequency vibration of their field.

Sherra "A year ago, we had to have our Jack Russell Lucy, PTS. I was utterly distraught, as was my husband. The next day, praying for a sign from her, I was about to go outside, to sit with my husband. He said, shhhhhhhhhhh, and pointed to the mat. There was the most amazing red butterfly with black markings, gently flapping its wings, almost like a wave. It stayed there for a very long time! and then flew away. Suddenly our whole garden was full of butterflies and birds for the rest of the afternoon. I looked into the neighbor's garden and saw not a thing, it was amazing. On the first anniversary after she left, on the same mat, a pure white feather. I get things like this quite often. I feel quite blessed."

Like steam from a pond
Pet Spirits gently transition from their fur suits
into Living Energy...
Instantly
They are whole, healthy and healed!
as their Souls become one with your Heart,
now, forever and always!

After Death Signs
book by Brent Atwater
Dennis Vito Photographer

CANDLES

Many times when you're thinking about your pet and have lit a candle to honor them, the flame will very obviously flicker and sway with no air movement in the room. You think this is strange because there is ABSOLUTELY no air movement in the room. Your heart wonders if it's them.

Yes mam!

Cely from California wrote "Last night I lit a candle for my baby boy Muffin. I thought the best place to have the candle would be in my room. As I lay in bed I noticed that the flame was going crazy! Just as if Muffin was wagging his tail and fanning the flame. When I was about to fall asleep the candle began to glow intensely, so much so that I couldn't stop looking at it. I knew he was watching over me. Even today at work Muffin sent me another sign.

I found **a piece of his Fur (or whisker -another common Sign)** on a computer screen and he's been gone for several months. These Signs make me feel so much closer to him like he's telling me that he's fine and that he's also thinking of me!"

Spirits can also affect air movement, bursts of light and other non-tangible realities, because they are part of that non-tangible environment.

CLOUD and other FORMATIONS

Many pet parents find solace looking toward the sky for a Sign from their Pet. I am always amazed at the artistry and inventiveness animals display making their statements.

Sometimes when you have a favorite photo of your pet, they'll send you a cloud formation like or similar to the outline or image of that photo to be sure that you recognize it's them watching over you.

Julie's Sparky did a great job on arranging these cloud groupings to include even the tilt of her head and her light and dark coloration!

Mandy's Jay was super creative with this stain in the drawer.

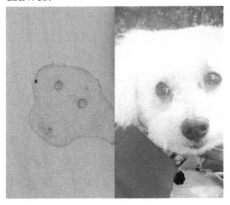

Mandy shared "Yesterday I went outside and sat next to my baby's grave to visit and talk to him. After talking with Jay for a while I asked "Can you hear me baby"?

I know he can and that he's always with me because I get Signs from him a lot- but I hadn't received any in a while. The next time I looked up there was his sweet little face right over me in the sky looking down at me. Then a few moments later there was a big J in the sky. He just amazes me. We always had such a strong connection and we still do. He always knows the right moments to show himself to me. If you ever doubt if they are listening. They are!"

Notice the detail facial features in the lower right photo above and in the other details, Jay is very artistic!

Faye "It was not too long after our St. Bernard Chia went to the Rainbow Bridge that she came to me in a dream. She was running across a most beautiful meadow ears flapping tongue hanging out and she started talking to me and could understand her perfectly. She said I am no longer in pain, I hurt nowhere any more. Said I have everything I need here but you. She said remember me and be happy.

That dream meant so much to me just wish she would come back again. Then on her way home from work Chia made another statement. Good dog

Your pet is ready, willing and able to add their special touch to your world so you'll know they are always listening and watching over you!

Diane asked Selena to send interesting cloud formations while she was sitting outside around sunset. The Phoenix came first. The clouds then changed into the Angel shape right before her eyes!
Just ask!

COINS

Pets are not limited to the items they send. Random **coins are always a favorite**. Usually money makes us feel more "valuable" via Earth standards. When coins cross your path know that your Pet values you in their life!

It's also interesting that a penny is 1, a universal symbol that everything is part of "all there is" or "oneness", i.e. no separation. 10 is the number of endings and new beginnings. Plus, coins are circular denoting complete balance, wholeness and a symbol of infinity with no beginning and no end!

Ms. Virga shared "Strange happenings this evening. First this penny showed up on my table. 2013=the year Selena transitioned. Next, I left my computer for a little while and when I returned this photo was open on top of the other Windows screen I had left open. (Taken 2-14-13). I hadn't been viewing photos, hadn't looked at this one in a while, and have no explanation."

This is a purrfect example of a Cat not only answering her Mom's request but also using electronic equipment to insure she made her point!

Some pets have a great sense of humor and sense of self. You may ask for a specific Sign and get something else!

Diane "This morning I asked my pet to send me a penny. No penny all day long, but this afternoon I found a lone dime on the closet floor while I was patching the wall in there. I guess she did it her way – Cattitude!"

Douglas states "my BAM sends coins, sometimes its quarters, nickels or dimes I find, almost always heads down."

Frankie writes "Yes they do send us coins! I find them often and one day I was kidding with Bear and said, "Okay, today how about a dime" ... I left the house to do some errands and when I came back there was a shiny dime placed directly in front of my laptop on the table. It was the spot where I had picked up my purse from when I left and there was nothing there. I live alone, so no one else placed it there right where I would see it. I love it! Be glad you are being blessed by your fur baby"

COINCIDENCES – NOT!

My Mike still sends Postcards and magazines on my birthdays and major holidays. Animals in Heaven also craft special somethings when you least expect it!

Nancy shared "We moved a lot. My job had me traveling across the country. Rizzo would fly with me. I would always tell him "We're going on another adventure." As he was passing, I was holding and telling him that he would have to go on this new adventure alone and I would eventually join him.

146

A few days after this we were driving along and of course I was thinking of him. For no reason, I just happened to look up and see only half of a billboard. Normally I pay no intention to them but this one I couldn't ignore. In big letters it said: IN TRANSITION, CONTINUE YOUR ADVENTURE. I could not tell you what the billboard was about because that is all I saw of it, but I knew inside of me that I was what I was meant to see.

There are times when something happens that you think, hmm that's interesting and then there are things that happen and you know it is for a reason because it speaks to your soul.
Rizzo spoke to my Soul that day."

Kristina adds "My Cosmo (cat) transitioned earlier this month. I have been grieving and wanting a sign so badly, that I think it's been tough for him to get through. A couple days ago, I decided enough sitting home feeling bad and decided to take my kids to go pick strawberries. Through a series of coincidences, we didn't get to the farm in time to pick strawberries before they closed and ended up going somewhere else completely unplanned.

I don't know how it happened, but my GPS led us to a garden store while we were looking for the farm. Driving by this store, I was overcome by the presence of Cosmo. It was so sudden and unexpected but it made me stop and pay attention. I felt like I was exactly where I needed to be.

I took my kids to look at the beautiful ponds and fountains and told them that we would look for something to plant in honor of Cosmo. I don't know very much about plants, but the first one I was drawn to a plant called "Cat's meow." I know this is my Sign because I can just feel in my heart that it was not just a simple coincidence."

Marilyn wrote "A close friend asked for my help to set up a garden memorial for her Golden Retriever "Flash" that passed 4 years ago. My Lab Cheyenne and Flash were buddies in life. My friend insisted on flowers that were the color of her dog. We decided to pick the coneflowers together. Then she stopped and shouted oh Marilyn LOOK what the flower tag says...."CHEYENNE SPIRIT".

Wow, we both had TEARS IN OUR EYES. The tag also said it was a "Companion Flower". When her dog passed, she was followed around by an orange butterfly, her coat color. The flower tag also said, "It attracts butterflies." Hope you love the new memorial Flash and Cheyenne, thanks for the "Hello."

Brent Atwater's
Just Plain Love® Books presents

Sen's dog Fred is a multifaceted Sign sender.
"It's been over 2 months since my dog Fred passed away. We received the first Sign from him, **he turned on the ceiling light** around 6 in the morning, then 2 days later, I received a **feather.** I asked for Signs from him if he was with me when hiking. Then there were **3 moths** flying along with me and one of them landed on my shirt. The following week, I was driving and a **green grasshopper** landed on my car and it follows me all the way home. This past weekend a **dragonfly** landed on my hand while swimming in the lake" what am I to make of all these Signs?
A: Fred is very determined to let you know that he is with you everywhere!

Lori wrote "When my Macavity James crossed over 2 months ago, I lost my love but also lost my garbage can tipper. Yesterday, I came into my kitchen after **hearing a crash and my garbage can was tipped over**! It was nearly empty, thank goodness. I knew it was my boy's way of visiting me. Then, I went to my car to go out and when I started the engine, **my song for him was playing,** "this is my heartbeat song and I'm gonna play it..." It was very comforting and I smiled for a long while. I love you Macavity."

How will I know if it's my Pet?

Follow your heart,
you can't miss them!

Anne - "I was wondering about **temperature changes** and being visited by ones that have passed. I'm a musician and was playing a song that made me think of our dear dog. The thermostat went down a degree as I was playing a song, then up, and then down on another one. I remember viewing Brent's video that said when trying to feel their pet's energy that one will eventually feel a cool or pulsating air sensation. Has anyone else experience this or something similar?"

A: Spirits from the Other Side can cause the temperature in the room to drop, that's why oftentimes people feels chills being around "ghost" electromagnetic energy.

Rebekah noticed "Had a sign from Forrest this morning. Went to bed so sad and had another sob fest. In order to fall asleep, I often listened to podcasts. I put Brent's Pet Life Radio podcasts on, and fell asleep. I woke up this morning to the sound of her voice talking about Forrest. Ha ha. Wasn't MY Forrest she was talking about, but still -- how many dogs out there have that name? Felt like he was letting me know he is with me and not to be so sad."

A: YES –It was a subtle way of letting you know he was with you!   Forrest, shown above, is the pet mentioned in my Podcast. While watching Forrest in a Reading, he actually tested going over the death line and had "demands" before he went and THEN, tested out his new Sparkler form by doing whirlies and loop de loops!

Pets send Signs via random, song lyrics, TV ads, all sorts of "this couldn't be a coincidence" kind of things.

A Soul pet never dies
They just change forms.
They're beside you,
sending Signs and
watching over you
every breath you take.
Ask Them for guidance,
YOU are Their assigment
for Eternity!

After Death Signs
Book by Brent Atwater

CRYING is the #1 Sign that deceased Pets or Pet Spirits send!

Your Heart dog/ cat or Soulmate pet fur child is part of the fabric of your being. EVERY TIME They are near to you, around you, touch or tug on your energy field your heart responds. In the beginning its with tears! DURING your worst crying spell, it's a Sign that "Fluffy" is close to you, hugging you and letting you know that He/ She loves you. FYI, you're now continuing your Never-Ending Love together in a new way! Say "**Glad you're here- let's talk!**

DRAGONFLIES are one of the Universal symbols for positive change in your world and within yourself.

© Readwave.com

Another personal example, when Mike passed way, I had both a hummingbird and a dragonfly at different times follow me from room to room and stare at me through the windows and glass doors. At first, I thought they were mentally challenged (as in psycho-they were literally scaring me with their behavior). Then one day it dawned on me (I was a slow learner while experiencing deep grief), Hmmm- what if it might be Mike coming to watch over me and say hello. The moment I acknowledged and said "Hello Mikey," the dragonfly flittered up and down and the hummingbird danced in little circles and flew away.

NEVER doubt what your Heart knows to be true even if it's in a new Form or creative expression for a Sign that initially *really* stretches your awareness.

An example from a group member: "There are a few weird things that have happened and I'm now questioning whether I'm crazy or not. When listening to Brent's Pet Loss Radio podcast about getting over the guilt, I was crying and then noticed a **dragonfly** flew into my garage, landed at my feet, and stayed there until the podcast was over. Could this be my pet?" A: Yes!

Iris had a wonderful story "I had a beautiful dragonfly land on my shoulder and I got this feeling it was my baby Bear. I don't know if it was because I am hoping and my head is playing games with me- but that dragonfly stayed with me for about 30 minutes. I was talking to it like it was my baby Bear and I feel in my heart that it was."

This was not wishful thinking. Iris's Soul recognized the energy of her beloved Bear.

FYI "Dragonflies ask you to pay attention to to 'what you think is directly proportionate to what you have.' Dragonflies are the essence of the winds of change, messages of wisdom and communication. To see a dragonfly in your dreams symbolizes change and regeneration, and that something in your life is not as it appears.

Examine Dragonfly Signs to glean the fullness of the message your pet is imparting to you. Dragonflies also oftentimes announce the reincarnation process process in collaboration with many other Signs.

DREAM VISITS

Dream Visits come in all forms. Use the Prayer on page 80 to ask for Dream Visits. For answers to specific questions use the Prayer on page 81.

Some people believe that only good dreams have merit. However, even sad dreams have a message that is addressing a subject your Pet wants you to know about. Some dreams are just replays of your mental fears or shine a light on emotional issues surrounding your pet's Transition. Pay attention to all dreams. In time, like a puzzle, you'll see the whole picture. Dreams don't have an expiration date. You can dream about the same subject until you transition.

Pauline from Tenn. shared with us "Last night before I closed my eyes to sleep, I asked my precious girl Emmi to let me feel her presence if her Spirit was still around. Well I didn't feel anything but I said I love her then went to sleep. SHE SHOWED UP IN MY DREAM!!!!! This is the first time I dreamed of her since she transitioned two and a half months ago. In the dream, she came back to me as herself in the flesh. I got to hold her in my arms and kissed her and smelled her scent and loving on her. I didn't let her paws touch the ground and carried her everywhere with me. I fed her pieces of good treats. I woke up with a clear memory of the most joyous moments in the dream. I had a big smile on my face and I said Thank You for visiting me!"

From India Indrani emailed "When my baby Buchu passed away I was torn apart. I kept crying and talking to his photograph that if I could cuddle him once more. The next night in my dreams and I could touch him and cuddle him.

The very next day I saw a dog who was identical to Buchu with a couple in my neighborhood park. I was stunned as if I was seeing Buchu alive and running and playing. The dog's name was Sheru and I asked the couple if I could play with him and I played with him for an hour. Was so moved by this gesture sent by my fur baby, can't thank him enough."

"I dreamed my fur Baby Buchu came to me in his full form, cuddled with me, played with my other 2 dogs. I asked him how & where he was, he said he was with me and I could touch him whenever I wanted."

Julie wrote "The night Sam passed away; I had a vivid dream where he was in some sort of hospital being looked after. There were people like Drs and nurses, who told me he would not recover and I should decide what to do. I went into the room and he could speak, so I asked him what he wanted me to do. He told me he wanted to be free, so I told the people just that. He then changed into a fox and I saw him walk across a meadow into some trees, but he paused before leaving, turned and looked at me. The dream ended." I'm waiting to see that Fox! "

Michelle "About 9 years ago, our buddy Fred transitioned and that day and for several days after I would dream and see him in the house. **I would also feel him hit the bed like he did when he was alive**. That was his thing... to run his face up and down the side of the bed. Still makes me laugh. Now it's been years since anything has happened from Fred till about 2 months ago.

At the end of February Fred began showing up in my dreams for the first time in year!   I also felt him hit the bed as he used to. There were actually a couple dreams with Fred and Wilma together. Before Fred transitioned He and Wilma were together about 4 years. He was 14 and she 4...Wilma transitioned last week and I expected to see her and be visited in dreams like Fred did. To my surprise, it was Fred that showed up to let us know he's taking care of Wilma."

When Pets have a very connected relationship and one crosses over, then the remaining animal transitions, don't be surprised if both come to visit. Usually the pet that was the first to leave will be present during the Earth pet's transition to accompany them across to Rainbow Bridge. Andrew's Mother who lives in the USA dreamed of

Luna as a black and white cat with angel wings before she visited Japan. Immediately upon arrival, she saw a store displaying an umbrella imprinted with a winged black and white cat. Hello from Luna!

ELECTRONIC SIGNS

Those who've lost a cherished companion often report receiving a wide variety of electronic signs such as lights or lamps blinking on and off, radios and televisions turning on and off and displaying static or blank snow screens. Stereos, mechanical objects, phones, cell phones, computers and toys being activated "out of the blue"- literally, and other electromagnetic occurrences where "things that go haywire." These are normal activities.

Messages sometimes show up on computer screens, (read the incident under Coins) photos that you have not "pulled up" or lost -suddenly appear, texts "just happen," telephone answering machines play synthesized messages, odd recorded sounds and "white noise." Other electronics and appliances appears to be experiencing "interference." It's easy for a Spirit to affect electromagnetic devices because they are now in electromagnetic energy form too!

FYI Cats are extremely sensitive to energy. You'll see a cat lay on the chest heart area of a person who is sad or perhaps going through a divorce, or cuddling next to the area of your body that is experiencing a health issue. Like an Empath, many cats "take on" the negative energy of their pet parents, and can die from overexposure while trying to use their body as an energy dialysis for yours. Therefore, it's easy for our felines to use their sensitivity and manipulation of energy to message you!

Sarah texted "I did want to share this... He passed Friday 6/12. Saturday a photo popped into my my phone of him. I swear I never saw it before or took it. I only talked to 2 people about all this and neither sent/ emailed/ texted any photos (one does not know how even). I checked and triple checked to make sure all my prior photos and none are there of this. I would have remembered it. The photo was rather foggy like and very strange looking. Like almost not even fully processed. He is lying almost asleep. And OMG... it is actually dated 6/13. The day after he died. I swear it just 'appeared'. Okay call me strange but I do believe it is a Sign. He is telling me no matter the concerns or fears in his passing all is okay and I must live in the good we had and not be sad. It was his time. My one friend of the two I can talk to is a pet rescuer. I sent it to her and immediately she said as I felt that it is some sort of Sign."

Julie says "When I was ironing today, **the radio switched itself off as well,** which had never happened before. I don't know if any of these things mean anything, but Sam did pass on the anniversary of my grandmother's passing 9 years ago. I have been asking her and him to be close to me and to let me know that he is ok. It may a coincidence that all of these things have happened since he passed, but it doesn't feel that way. It feels deeply peaceful and reassuring and that there is something letting know that he is at peace and well."

For YEARS, Mike would always **ring the phone** once before I would go to sleep each night!

Amanda "Several times the TV turned itself off, or back on, from being off. The computer rebooted itself for no reason. After one day of happenings with the TV, I woke up at 2:25am to go to the toilet. I noted that the clock radio registered this time. Also, when I would awaken during the night I noticed that the clock radio was blinking on and off. It's interesting because there was no power outage that night."

FYI   when you add the Time numbers together is makes 9. In numerology, the number 9 is the number of Universal love, eternity, faith, Universal Spiritual Laws, the concept of karma, spiritual enlightenment, spiritual awakening, service to humanity, light working and lightworkers, life purpose and soul mission, intuition, and strength of character plus lots more. In addition to flicking the clock, Winston was sending another message to Mom! What a wonderful boy.

FYI A great book for the meaning of numbers is Healing with the Angels by Doreen Virtue.

Noreen "2 days after I lost my dog Kasey, I was texting a friend telling her that Kasey had such a loving a soul. As I hit send on my phone, the lights went out and came back on.

Later that day I was getting ready to go out and I wanted to wear a pair of heart earrings that I haven't worn in a year. Went to my jewelry box, only one was there. I decided to choose another pair as I didn't have time to search. Went to my kitchen, was about to leave and I started to talk to Kasey like I always did before I left the house. "Mama loves you so much, and I miss you so much." Thru my tears I noticed something on kitchen floor. The other heart earring! I haven't worn those earrings in a year and I sweep my kitchen floor every day.

She is definitely still with me!"

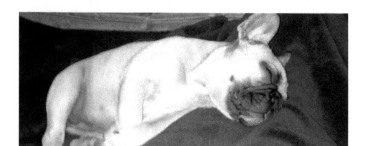

ENERGY PRESENCE

Prayer for Energy Presence page 85. More
commands under the Visitation section.

When a pet shows up as an Energy Presence i.e. a Pet Spirit, that's a Level 1 appearance. A random and quick Glitter Sparkle form visitation is Level 2. It usually precedes a full Level 3 Vision or Spirit Visitation which requires the most amount of electromagnetic manipulation on your animal's part.

Ask these Questions during any Visit

* Are you here for my Highest and best Good?
* Who are you?
* Who do you work for?
* Why are you here?
* What do you want me to know?
* Show me what you want me to know now.

They will answer you telepathically or you'll have a translatable feeling in your heart.

Many times, individuals are so rattled by a Visitation that they think it's not controllable. **It is!**

*** You can ask your pet to extend their Visitation for a period of time either specifically or as they so choose. When I do a Reading, I ask them to stay until all the questions are answered. In almost 20 years I've only had 2 Cats walk out early.

Remember to ask!

Individuals often "feel" or sense / recognize the energy presence of their dogs and cats as they lay in their lap or jump up on the bed each night like Mary would feel Rhett Butler do.

Some pets continue to sleep with their person long after their biological body has been discarded, even right up until they begin reentry. I felt Electra my "Squirrel girl" pressing close to my side when I was extremely upset and during summer "boomies" (thunderstorms).

Ann said "she has visited me on two occasions getting up on the bed and walking around me, you could feel the electrical energy, and I kid you not it felt like pins and needles each place she walked. I am so glad I found your group to talk about this. My Maya was the love of my life."

Sally said "I could swear I see my little Evita out of the corner of my eye for very brief moments. She always slept with me and sometimes I can feel her curled up beside me."

Louise added "Whenever I would see a butterfly or a bird, I can't help but feel that Ginny is visiting us. At one time, while I was half asleep on the couch, I felt that I was being licked on my left cheek and lips by Ginny.

When I opened my eyes, I was expecting to see Harry, my living dog. But to my surprise, Harry was fast asleep right by my feet. It was then that I realized that it was Ginny who was "kissing" me, and I truly felt this in my heart."

Heather "I have days where I feel her and have heard her meow and purr on several occasions. I'm comforted knowing she is with me.!!!"

Lenita "I've had the most amazing connection with my dear little Annie who transitioned 3 months ago. I've had lots of messages and signs from her and I have even felt her presence many times. Today I tried Brent's techniques, wow; it just blew me away... I asked Annie to lie in my lap and rest her head on my left arm as she so often did. I wasn't expecting anything the first time but even as I was saying my prayer and asking her to do this I could sense her around me. I had Goosebumps and felt cold. I knew she was with me. Then the most amazing thing... I felt warmth on my lap and I felt a sense of weight on my lap and arm. It felt so good. I'm so happy."

Danika "I talk to her every single night before I go to sleep and ask her for a Sign. The last Sign I got was amazing. When I was tossing and turning in bed, I felt her presence wrap herself around my head. It was her favorite place to sleep. It was AMAZING!"

Vera and Robert told me "Bentley (featured below) walked across the bed this morning at 3:45am. I saw his beautiful body walking by. He looked as magnificent as ever. I looked to my right a moment after he left to be sure I wasn't mistaken and there was our other cat Winston sleeping with his legs stretched out... Hello Bentley, YAY!!!

Later that day, Robert and I were talking and he said he also felt Bentley walk past our heads and he recognized the stride and pace of steps as those of Bentley. Robert never opened his eyes, but knew by the stride that it was not Winston walking past. It truly was a fantastic experience!"

FEATHERS

Feathers are a significant Spiritual sign. White feathers are said to come from the Wings of Angels. There's also an old saying "When Angels are near feathers appear."

Did you know that Native Americans believed that feathers represented communication with the Spirit world? They also believed finding a feather was a sign of new beginnings and rebirth of Spirit.

When you find a feather in an inappropriate place, it's a nice reminder that you're being thought of by your pet from Above at Pet Heaven or Rainbow Bridge.

Jessica from Singapore writes "I've recently lost my dear bunny about 2 months ago, and was sobbing my eyes out when I found a small white feather at the exact spot he passed away. I stay in a high-rise apartment in Singapore (where I can't fathom how a white feather gets here because there are no chickens/white birds around) and it's the first time I've ever seen it and I want to thank Churros."

Although it's always important to listen to your inner guidance, after the loss of a pet, it may be your fur baby redirecting your routine in order to find that special message.

Anne emailed "Something made me take the stairs instead of the elevator today and I found a white feather after the first flight of them. Every sign means so much. I'm glad I listened to my inner guidance."

Kerry wrote "Today marks one month since I lost Jessie. Each day she has presented me with a feather and even another white feather at my feet today"

Trista "Found a small white feather next to my car when I was leaving work to go home. It is a windy day and it just sat there, unable to be moved by the wind. Just like my bond and love for Daytona, my kitty, our love and bond are untouchable, strong and everlasting."

Victoria texted, "I find feathers every day and have quite a pile of them. I have started finding smaller white feathers with half of the feather missing, meaning that the bottom half is heart shaped and I hear & feel him purring."

Valerie added more "Feathers, feathers everywhere!!! I got in my car yesterday morning to find a feather gently lying on my wiper blade; I laughed & took it into my car. When I got home, there was a tan & white feather (Benny's colors) on my mailbox. Then today, while cutting Spritzer's nails,

I noticed a tiny downy one stuck to her foot! So many signs! They make me smile!"

Amanda "This morning before I got out of bed I was talking to Winston. I asked if he could give me a message today to let me know that he was okay and happy. I said that the sign would be a feather. A feather would mean that he is ok and happy and can hear me. When I got to work, Robyn announced that she had bought a goose feather down quilt.

I cannot remember the last time I heard someone say the word feather. Then this afternoon, I was walking across the front lawn and saw a small white and grey coloured feather. About 30 minutes later I saw another larger grey feather.   I cannot recall the last time I saw a feather on the ground, so not a likely coincidence. It was definitely a message from Winston, as I had asked. Thank you, my sweetheart."

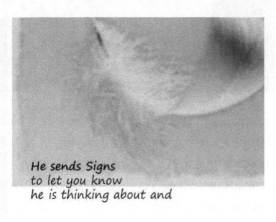

He sends Signs
to let you know
he is thinking about and

Leanne "I was teaching my toddler who everyone in the family was, through pictures I'd put on the fridge. When I asked him to point to Jessie (our bird who'd recently passed) he pointed to top of the chair right behind me. I asked him if Jessie was sitting there and he said yes! He would also see her flying through the house and would follow her.

She was unable to fly when he knew her; because of a disability...knowing that she was flying in Spirit was very comforting. I also had a white feather follow me around wherever I'd go - the same feather! I'd be outside and it would be on my blanket, I'd come inside and it would be on the couch. Jessie, in her new incarnation, will be white. That's my girl!"

John shared "This morning as I was listening to songs about departed Pets and feeling very sad. I got up to go to the kitchen from my bedroom to get another cup of coffee, as I got to my door, on the ground; I found this one little feather of a small bird. I looked for a reason why this would be in my room. Then I got a real warm loving feeling in me that made me cry. I then realized it must have been a gift from my little boy Poopy. It made me happy."

Brent Atwater's
Just Plain Love® Books presents

FLOWERS

From the United Kingdom Vicky says "Just after my Kola transitioned I went on a vacation to get me out of the house and away to help me deal with my loss. I was most distraught the whole time I was away. One day I took myself for a walk. I was asking Kola over and over to send me a sign he was ok and was with me and that he knew I missed him. I asked for something specific either to send me a pink rose or a heart or a feather. As I carried on my walk a lady came out of a florist with a very impressive bouquet of flowers and as she walked by one fell to the ground. I bent down to pick it up for her and she said 'oh dear, you must keep that one. It was obviously meant for you!!!' It was a very beautiful pink rose!!! I know it was my sign from my Kola."

"Later on, in the next few months, I went out to tidy up my garden. I had been putting off doing my garden time. To me it was me and Kola time. I was so sad and near to tears when I was pruning my favourite plant. I had planted it the same time I got Kola, so it always reminded me of him. When I got to the base I found a heart shape card. I know it was his sign to me.

Also, that year the very plant I had for eight years (same time I had Kola) died shortly after I found the heart. Even stranger I placed that heart on a beautiful orchid and the orchid is also no more"

From India Sneha "saw a feather in midst of flower garden as if it was just kept for me to see. And then Apple trees where they should not have been. My Mitthu could not do without apples. Even on his last physical day, all he had was apples."

From Oregon Daryl wrote "Back when we were together in the physical form, Hunter and I would pass by a plant like this one nearly every day while out on the walk. He wasn't terribly interested in it, but the gardener/ plant lover in me sure was. I would halt our walk and admire this plant and wonder what it was. I couldn't identify it and I wanted one for my garden.

Sometime after Hunter transitioned, one of these plants appeared in my garden. I was thrilled and had no doubt of who had planted it there. A month later, two more showed up in the front garden. I have checked around the neighborhood and our garden is the only one that has these plants in it. This has been the clearest message from Hunter that I have received. He knows I have put a lot of energy into attempting to contact him. Hunter is indeed the being who is responsible for my quest into Spirit."

His Soul begins
the search
for
the Haven of
your heart.

HEARTS

Nothing symbolized Love more than a heart shape. Animals are ingenious at sending "I love you" Mom or Dad Signs via all sorts of methods.

William told us "Right after the passing of my beautiful Border Collie, Maia Lyn, I received several Signs in the form of hearts. Most were somewhat faint and not easy to see. About a month after her passing I had not seen anything for a while. I spent 2 very bad days crying my eyes out. I was not asking for a Sign, I thought those were over with. I went outside that evening to take our other other dogs for their evening bathroom break, as I turned to go back in the house, I happened to look down on our fire pit and noticed this amazing heart in the snow... my heart jumped, I knew beyond a doubt that my Maia Lyn was still with me."

Dianne "Most of my signs have come in the form of heart-shaped rocks. I still find them directly in my path almost every day, especially at the beach. My friends enjoy the fact that I find so many. I think this is one of the most beautiful, found in my yard."
FYI, she has 100's!!!!!!!

Adam wrote "After what seems like a while of not receiving any signs from Bessie, I find this. I was walking and stopped for a second and something told me to look down and this heart shaped rock was right at the tip of my foot. It sure brought a smile to my face."

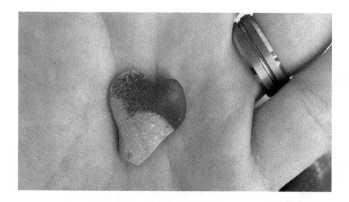

"This fur heart made me laugh out loud: a heart-shaped "dust bunny", complete with cat hair. Selena is showing me a sense of humor I didn't know she had. Yes, I know I need to vacuum, my sweet girl!"

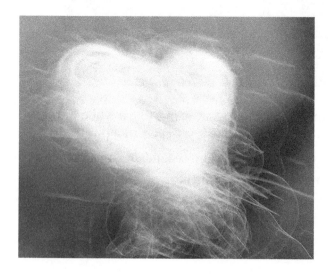

Aussie Melissa "My sign before my girl returned were clouds in the shape of hearts.... Now I have my girl back and she has a heart in the middle if her forehead!!!! And her name is Cloud!!! I feel the hole in my heart has gone! She is back where she belongs to enjoy thus journey with us and the kids!!!!"

Many people take their heart shaped collections of rocks, coral or shells and create an altar, candle dish, waterfall, garden wall or other "places" symbolic of all the loved shared with their pet or in places they loved together.

"I went to the feed store today to buy cat and dog food. I go every weekend and since Bear passed, I miss buying "his" food that he liked. I was thinking of him and missing him as I was leaving the store. I don't ever look at mud puddles, but this one made my head turn to look at it as I was leaving the parking lot."

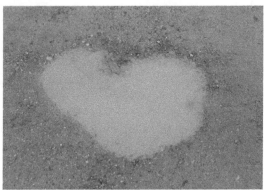

HUMMINGBIRDS

The Hummingbird represents the enjoyment of life and lightness of being. It encourages you to develop your adaptability and resiliency while still keeping a playful and optimistic outlook toward life. They are often seen interchanged with Dragonflies. Hummingbirds also represent change is coming.

GLITTER or *SPARKLER FORM

Usually the Glitter or Sparkler form precedes you seeing a full Spirit Visitation vision. Some pet parents only get to this level of Visitation. Either way, once you have accomplished Level 2 you can always reaccess it and can use the same questioning techniques for an Energy Presence Visitation.

From Bulgaria Biryani adds "And then I woke up...outside was still dark...the special time before the dawn. I know it wasn't just a dream, it was a visit and a sign...He was so alive, so himself, so full of energy but there was something around him as a subtle glitter. And what I find really cute is that he didn't look younger and had all the battle marks on his nose, the torn ears, - just as he was... :)))

His Soul is **always** by your side.

Jessica asks "Then I asked for a sign from her while in my car and the song, "wait for me to come home" came on. The last weird thing is for the last year I've been seeing sparkles.... like glitter in the air. It only lasts a few seconds, but it usually happens when I'm quiet and calm. The weird thing that made me think it might be connected is that Brent calls the animal spirit their sparkler form. Just thought I would see what you all might think."

A: Definitely a Sparkle Visitation and not weird at all. Tell her to keep on visiting!

"I celebrate your Love and set my Grief free, so You can choose to come back to me!"

Could you please be a little smaller in our next
Lifetime together?

MOVING OBJECTS

A friend recently lost her gorgeous Springer Spaniel.
Always a bargain hunter, she found a fabulous
English porcelain plate with a Springer Spaniel
puppy on it in a Consignment shop. Looking at the
plate touched her heart and she immediately
purchased it!

As she was getting back into her car while adjusting her purse and keys, that plate slipped out of her hands and shattered on the asphalt.

Why? Roux's living energy was so strong that he caused the place to be dislodged from her hand because he does not want her to look at that plate and continue to grieve for him.

Pets can create nudgies, bursts of air, and things that go bump, be thankful they are trying to get your attention to say "Hi!" When you are crying nonstop, praying or just wondering if your beloved "family member" is okay, sometimes your pet will cause a commotion or distraction that you recognize in your heart is their response letting you know they're fine!

Revel would use his energy to knock his pictures off the bedside table when Kim was upset or crying. He let her know that he was right there with her!

IF something is moving without you know ing why, ASK who is creating the motion and what they want you to know. Most times it's your pet- just say your Protection Prayer to be sure!

NUMBERS & NUMBER SEQUENCES

Carol wanted us to know "A few weeks ago, while walking the road we always walked with Gracie, we came upon a five-dollar bill just lying there. Picked it up and trusted that it was a sign from Gracie. I talk to Gracie all the time though she hasn't come to my dreams. Today I was asking her if and when she might come back. At that moment, I passed a house address I was drawn to while driving down this rural road -- 1445 -- which adds up to five in numerology. Later I remembered the five-dollar bill and now I am wondering if there might be a link."

A: Five is the number representing Change

One of my Favorite resource books for Numerology is **Healing with the Angels by Doreen Virtue**. It has a section that explains what various number sequences mean and for me it is 100% correct. Fascinating!

Be alert to REOCCURRING number sequences anywhere! Radios, license plates, addresses, phone numbers, they usually contain a message to think about.

Valery shared "I understand that the dates on coins could represent when they leave us or relate to their age, the year we adopted them, etc. but what about coins whose dates seemingly have no connection to the pet? Deirdre's penny was dated 1972. Long time ago! I added the numbers together and it comes out 19 or 1 + 9 = 10. I cannot think of how that might relate to her."

A: Ten is the number of endings and new beginnings!

ORBS

An Orb is a circular ball of electromagnetic mass that is a singular energy entity and energy form classification unto itself. Pet Spirits often use Orb forms to visit. Orbs are usually seen at twilight and later. White orbs are positive energy and respond to love and happy places and occasions. They even emit their own electronic sounds and show up quite often in photographs.

Frankie sent us this "Just the other day, I took photos of Tia "hanging out" in my office with me. She wasn't the only one that was enjoying the sofa. Love you Bear Man."

Orbs can also let you know Your Pet's energy is with you BEFORE their arrival on Earth in a Physical Form.

Announcing a Future Presence

Look at the face in the orb which appeared a few years BEFORE the Dog on the following page arrived. She was checking out her surrounding and letting her Mom know she was on the way!

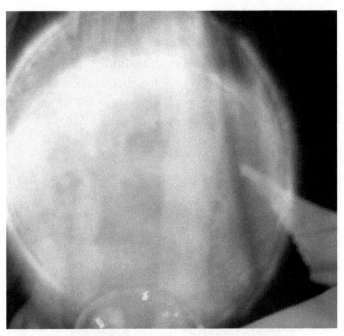

Orbs can also denote a Pets visit to their special place. Selena's Orb visited her Garden spot on multiple occasions after her transition.

When Jessie the Cockatiel was alive, she liked to sit on Dwayne's shoulder; it was one of her special places. After she transitioned she continued to do so in Orb form.

PHOTOS and VIDEOS

A pet may insert their previous image, an Orb, or their steam form into any photo or video you or someone else took so the finished picture will be something entirely different! That's another "Hello!" When in doubt – ASK who it is!

This photo Sign was sent from a Pet at Rainbow Bridge to his Beloved Companion still on Earth.

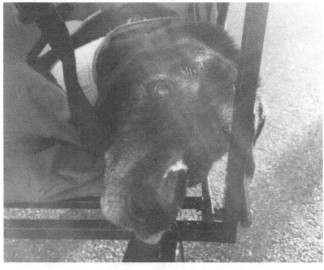

One of our Pet Group members shared a Video that she had taken to show the new décor in her remodeled Kitchen. Lo and behold her dog's Spirit was walking around on film! We all were amazed!

RAINBOWS

Rainbows are the # 2 SIGN that lets you know your pet is NOT dead and waiting for you at Rainbow Bridge. They are telling you I'm alive, healthy, happy and waiting to begin our new journey together in Pet Spirit form so we can continue our never-ending love!

Remember, factually, Rainbow Bridge is a mythical place, a make-believe Pet Heaven created by a poem written around 1980's.

Jeannine "One night on the year anniversary of Toby's transition, I was waiting for a sign, anything, about 530 that evening I was complaining to my husband how upset I was that I didn't get anything. Not a song, a penny, no dream the night before. After my rant, I picked up my new dog and from my door a HUGE rainbow appeared in the sky. It wasn't there minutes earlier, I knew it was Toby."

Ms. Sawert wrote "It's been a while since I received a sign but this morning I saw a very vibrant rainbow then a while later I heard our song on the radio. Thanks Baxter, my special boy. He hasn't forgotten me after all."

Rainbow Signs are NOT limited to the Sky. That image can be on trucks, pages in a book, on T shirts and lots more depending upon your pet's creativity. Theresa also shared "A truck with a rainbow on it from a company 2 hrs. away, parked across the road for a day for no reason. I knew it was Baxter."

Believe in your Pet's
Return from Rainbow Bridge

Return from Rainbow Bridge Poems and Videos

For those that embrace the belief of Animal Life after death and Reincarnation we have a series of Poems (for dogs, cats, horses, shelter pets, special needs animals etc.) on my website. Each poem is translated into many languages www.BrentAtwater.com.

You are welcome to download a copy and to share with others. They are free.

Our Return from Rainbow Bridge Videos are translated into multiple languages on YouTube.

Return from Rainbow Bridge for Cats

When a Cat dies his Soul transitions to a special place in Heaven
called the Rainbow Bridge.
There He is alive and well, a part of Never Ending Love.
He is healed, whole, and restored to purrfection.

He meets special friends and head bumps loved ones.
They run, play, clean and cuddle together.
There is plenty of food, water and sunshine.
Everyone is warm, safe and comfortable.

He visits you in dreams with memories of the special times you shared.
He is happy and content EXCEPT for one thing.
He misses that special bond with the person he had to leave behind.
He sends signs to let you know he is thinking about and watching over you.
His Soul is ALWAYS by your side.
He has NEVER stopped loving you!

Then the day comes when your Cat wants to be back.
There are promises to keep.
He quivers and sparkles with intent.
It's time to return to Earth as you both have agreed.
His energy vibrates faster and faster,
forming a Heart to be loved.

He feels the pull of your Prayers and yearnings.
He is strengthened by the power of your belief in Never Ending Love.
Full of Hope and Faith he leaves the safety of Rainbow Bridge.
His Soul begins the search for the Haven of your heart.

In perfect timing that moment arrives.
You find one another!
Time stands still as you look into each other's Soul.

Your heart is etched with the feeling of recognition in his eyes.
Cautiously you move forward filling the gaps that complete your bond.
Your touch caresses his beloved velvet head.
All sadness is gone.
Your heart is whole again!

Your Cat has returned from the Rainbow Bridge.
Together you begin again,
another journey
in the Eternal Cycle of Life!
Your Love is here

a Dog's Return from Rainbow Bridge

When a Dog dies his Soul transitions to a special place in Heaven
called the Rainbow Bridge.
There He is alive and well, a part of Never Ending Love.
He is healed, whole, and restored.

He sniffs special friends, meets family and hugs loved ones.
They chase one another, play and bark together.
There is plenty of food, treats, chewies, balls, bones and sunshine.
Everyone is warm, safe and comfortable in their beds.

He visits you in dreams with memories of the special times you shared.
He is happy and content EXCEPT for one thing.
He misses that special bond with the person he had to leave behind.
He sends signs to let you know he is thinking about and watching over you.
His Soul is ALWAYS by your side.
He has NEVER stopped loving you!

Then the day comes when your Dog wants to be back.
There are promises to keep.
He wiggles and sparkles with intent.
It's time to return to Earth as you both have agreed.
His energy vibrates faster and faster,
forming a Heart to be loved.

He feels the pull of your Prayers and yearnings.
He is strengthened by the power of your belief in Never Ending Love.
Full of Hope and Faith he leaves the safety of Rainbow Bridge.
His Soul begins the search for the Haven of your heart.

In perfect timing that moment arrives.
You find one another!
Time stands still as you look into each other's Soul.

Your heart is etched with the feeling of recognition in his eyes.
Cautiously you move forward filling the gaps that complete your bond.
Your touch caresses his beloved velvet head.
All sadness is gone.
Your heart is whole again!

Your Dog has returned from the Rainbow Bridge.
Together you begin again,
another journey
in the Eternal Cycle of Life!
Your Love is here
Now,
Forever and Always!

A Shelter Pet's Return from Rainbow Bridge

My heart is warm and my spirit bold
I'll never have the chance to grow old.
Depressed and scared, no matter my age
I've been put in a death row cage

I've done my best to win your attention
now left behind in loveless detention
Abused, abandoned and soon I'll die
I didn't get adopted or rescued- Why?

Was I not pretty or healthy enough
Can't you see beyond that stuff?
Where is your help when I need you?

The gas burns my eyes and my lungs too
Killing me off from loving you

WOW! What a special place in Heaven
they call it the Rainbow Bridge.
I'm alive and well, a part of Never Ending Love.
My body is healed, whole, and restored.

Oh my! Special friends, family and loved ones are here.
There is plenty of food, toys and sunshine for me.
Everyone is warm, safe and has their own bed.

I still yearn for that special bond with my own person.
I promise,
my Soul will ALWAYS be by your side.
I'll NEVER abandon or stop loving you!

Then the day comes when
it's my time to return to Earth
Full of Faith and Love I leave the safety of Rainbow Bridge.
My Soul begins again the search for the Haven of your heart.

In perfect timing that moment arrives.
We find one another!

Everything stands still as we look into each other's Soul.
I pray that you will adopt me.
Your touch caresses my head.
Oh please oh please, pick me!
so my sadness will be gone
and my heart can be whole again!

Being wanted is FINALLY here
You're taking **ME!** I'm Homeless no more!
Together we begin as a forever family.
Now I'm Happy and LOVED!
and my Soul is at peace
in this Cycle of Eternal Life!

*****

213

Return from Rainbow Bridge for Horses

When a Horse dies his Soul transitions to a special place in Heaven
called the Rainbow Bridge.
There He is alive and well, a part of Never Ending Life.
He is healed, whole, sound and restored.

He meets special friends, family and loved ones. They nuzzle, play and graze together.
There is plenty of food, water, treats, salt licks and sunshine.
Everyone is warm, safe and comfortable.

He visits you in dreams with memories of the special times you shared.
He is happy and content EXCEPT for one thing.
He misses that special bond with the person he had to leave behind.
He sends signs to let you know he is thinking about and watching over you.
His Soul is ALWAYS by your side.
He has NEVER stopped loving you!

Then the day comes when your Horse wants to be back.
There are promises to keep.
He neighs, paws, snorts then quivers with intent.
It's time to return to Earth as you both have agreed.
His energy vibrates faster and faster,
forming a Heart to be loved.

He feels the pull of your Prayers and yearnings.
He is strengthened by the power of your belief in Never Ending Love.
Full of Hope and Faith he leaves the safety of Rainbow Bridge.
His Soul races to search for the Haven of your heart.

In perfect timing that moment arrives.
You find one another!
Time stands still as you look into each other's Soul.

Your heart is etched with the feeling of recognition and familiarity.
Cautiously you move forward filling the gaps that complete your bond.
As you look into large trusting eyes, feeling his warm breath on your face
your touch caresses his beloved head and hugs his silken neck.
All sadness is gone.
Your heart is whole again!

Your Horse has returned from the Rainbow Bridge.
Together you begin again,
another journey
in the Eternal Cycle of Life!
Your Love is here
Now,
Forever and Always!

A Special Need Pet's Return from Rainbow Bridge

My heart is warm and my spirit bold
will you give me a chance to grow old?
"Special" and scared, no matter my age
Please don't put me in a death row cage

How blessed I am to have you as mine.
This has to be a plan so divine
that you pray and tend my every need,
and for doing everything possible I'm grateful indeed!
Your nurturing vigilance keeps me alive
and your keeping me comforatble allows me to thrive.

The time and money you sacrifice for me
makes you an Angel it has to be!
Your extraordinary support is beyond compare
and I greatly appreciate that you're always there!

But now I must say good bye,
I've experienced unconditional love so don't you cry
Get some rest as I leave this Earth
Hold me in your heart until my rebirth.

WOW! What a special place in this Heaven
they call it the Rainbow Bridge.
I'm alive and well, a part of Never Ending Love.
My body is healed, whole, and totally restored.

Oh my! Special friends, family and loved ones are here.
There is plenty of food, toys and sunshine for me.
Everyone is warm, safe and has their own bed.

I still yearn for our special bond.
I promise,
My Soul will ALWAYS be by your side.
I'll NEVER abandon or stop loving you!

Now the day comes,
it's my time to return to Earth!
Full of Faith and Love I leave the safety of Rainbow Bridge.
My Soul begins the search for the Haven of your heart.

In perfect timing that moment arrives.
We find one another!
Time stands still as we look into each other's Soul.
Your touch caresses my head.

I pray you'll recognize my healthy new body
and listen to your heart's urgings
so my sadness is gone,
and your heart can be whole again!

Let's begin again,
this time, I'll take care of YOU!

Pet Spirits say
If Life turned upside down
when I left my Earth Suit

KNOW

I'm healthy, happy & healed
& with you
Forever & Always!

Brent Atwater the Animal Medium
www.BrentAtwater.com

REINCARNATION SIGNS

Then the day comes when your Pet wants to be back!

" Smitty" #1

Although only 30 to 40% of pets reincarnate to continue learning opportunities with you, sometimes animals get REAL blatant about letting you know they have returned and will be back in your arms soon. Learn more about reincarnation in my book Animal Reincarnation.

The MOST obvious Sign I have experienced is with Smitty. One week prior to return, his Mom was "directed" to go down a road after losing her map.

The Sign "Smitty did it!" just "happened "to be on the side of that road!

Days later, Pat was holding Smitty "2" in her arms!

SMELLS and SCENTS

Never discount Smells and Scents. Many times, they are the first after death transmission from the Other Side because it's easy for Spirit to change up the electromagnetic energy in the air. Since these signals are so subtle, individuals usually dismiss the odors as "a weird" coincidence. NOT!

Michelle added "Tonight while sitting on the bed

reading one of the books... my room smelled like dog. That "I need a bath smell". It's how Fred smelled sometimes. It was VERY distinct, and I knew it was Fred."

Sharon added "My dream was so real I could feel and smell my pet's fur. It happened to me last night."

Molly shared "I was at work and all of a sudden I smelled roses like I was surrounded by them. At the same time, I heard a chime and the words " Mom I'm coming home' and that was just the beginning of LOTS more Signs and Visitations!"

Pet parents also relate they smell their wet Labrador, dog passing gas, fur smells and other familiar odors. Your pet will always choose smells that you will recognize and can identify with a specific time in your life! Like humans, pets send scents from flowers, sweat, cologne and even Cigar smells that caused them to sneeze

SONGS and MUSIC

Together AGAIN in this Lifetime!

My Mike always played "Time, Love and Tenderness" by Michael Bolton. Before I understood this was a Sign, I wondered "why does that song play so much?" Pets will play your favorite song anywhere, anytime, or the song you used to sign to them. TV commercials at night before you go to bed can be a reminder he's watching over you. Never under estimate or doubt your pet!

Sally said "Then I asked for a sign from her while at work and in the elevator the song, "wait for me to come home" came on...not sure if it was coincidence or if it was her." A: Yes, if "it might be my pet"-it is!

FYI often times the VERY first song you hear when you turn the radio on is usually a message from Spirit when you have a loved one living on the Other Side.

Anne "It was three weeks ago today that my Sweet Sadie Girl transitioned. She was a stray that was with me only 5 short weeks. The instant connection I felt with her was magical. In a few short weeks, she will have been gone from me longer than she was with me. Our connection was so strong and I feel her all around me.

Each morning when I went into her room to feed her, I would turn the radio on. Almost each day I would hear the George Michael/Elton John song "Don't Let the Sun Go Down on Me". I would always sing it to her. I now continue to hear that song. I will never hear the song and not think of my Sadie Girl. I am hopeful that our paths will cross again soon."

Karen wrote "We rescued our sweet Maya 11 years ago from the streets of Belize and brought her back to the US to join our family. We found each other there in some Mayan ruins and knew we were meant to be together in this life.

Maya died suddenly of a pulmonary embolism. The day following her death, and in the grips of unbelievable grief, I was driving in my car thinking about an episode I had the night before (our first bedtime without her) where I got up in the middle of the night and I was looking all over the house for her and calling her name. I woke my husband up and asked him where she was. As I sat at the traffic light, I was wondering what caused me to do that. I must have been sleep walking or dreaming, but I remembered doing it.

As I'm thinking about this, the radio was on, but I wasn't listening. All of a sudden I became aware of the song lyrics, "Hey now, hey now.... don't dream it's over..."

At that very moment, I looked up at the intersection and I saw a van pass in front of me that had the words "Animal Services" and it had a big red paw print on the side of the van. I took that as confirmation that Maya sent me that message through the song lyrics."

Diane emailed "2 songs played on the radio while I was driving today and I felt them as Signs from Selena. The first was "Always and Forever", clearer than any other song that station played. The second began the instant I pulled out of a parking lot and it was "See You Again."

Christine shared "I had the Lean on Me song come on 3 days in row. I feel I need to lean on Winnie's strong spirit and energy to get through her loss. It helps me!"

Jackie said "I had an interesting sign from Fizzbin the past couple weeks. In the Reading he talked about me singing to him when he was quite young (keep in mind this would have been about 30 years ago) but he named the song "You Are My Sunshine"

Although I didn't have a clear memory of it in time I remembered the song. Within the last two weeks my daughter and I were shopping at a local store that had some shirts with paw prints and were pet themed. We were looking through them and there was a bright orange T-shirt in my size with a big paw print in the middle and believe it or not the words "You Are My Sunshine" printed on it!

I didn't buy the shirt at that time because orange isn't a color I normally wear much. But my husband and I were back at the same store and they had a clearance rack and yep, the shirt was STILL there so I thought maybe I was supposed to buy it as a continuous Sign from Fizzbin."

Dianne "While driving this song came on and I felt it was from Selena- Because You Love Me by Celine Dion -even before I remembered that my cat shares a version of her name. Right back at you, my girl. Later that day 2 songs played on the radio while I was driving home and I felt them as more Signs from Selena. The second began the instant I pulled out of a parking lot and it was "See You Again."

From Norway Isselin "My beautiful boy Fres gave me a song. The lyrics made me scream in pain and relief. When he passed, I got this urge to listen to music. I scrolled down the list and when I got to Stephen marley - hey baby I heard a major. It sounded like my Fres and when I heard the lyrics I knew my baby spoke to me. I try not to cry, I know he just want me happy and safe and I will try my hardest to get there."

Frankie "There are two songs I hear on the radio when I am feeling Bear close or just driving and ask for a Sign. Tonight, when I got in the car, the radio was playing I Love You Always Forever. I have a folder full of his signs and the way he communicates with me."

From Canada Timea wrote "I was out yesterday doing some shopping. I started crying in the car before heading into the drug store to get a shampoo. I asked Mario to send me a Sign because I am very very sad and miss him very very much. I walk into the store and within a minute the music changes. Suddenly a song I never heard in my life comes up.

And the guys start singing: I love you and I will always be with you no matter what, I will be waiting for you, right here right now. I will see you again, soon, I will come back to you......Needless to say I was like: huh? My cat just sent me a song?" A: Yes, he did!

Jeni said "while at the vet's office, I held her paws and whispered in her ear to 'come find me.' A few mornings later, I woke up with Tracy Chapman's song 'The Promise' in my head. Music has always had a purpose or a message for me. I immediately felt like Phoebe had head-bonked me."

Jessica "Then I asked for a Sign from her while in my car and the song, 'wait for me to come home' came on...not sure if it was coincidence or if it was her. The last weird thing - for the last year I've been seeing sparkles.... like glitter in the air. It only lasts a few seconds, but it usually happens when I'm quiet and calm. The weird thing that made me think it might be connected is that Brent calls the animal spirit their Sparkler form."

Trust and Believe! And remember "coming home" can mean in living Spirit form!

Vivian says "Two weeks ago, I helped my soul kitty transition. This decision, although I know was the best gift I could give him has been tearing my heart out. At the very end of a TV documentary

I was watching, a family is heard singing a song together. This song happened to be 'You are my sunshine,' which was my Ozzie's favorite song. He would pick his back legs up and dance when I sung it to him. I can't help but feel like he wanted me to watch that documentary so I can find peace in the final gift I gave him when I hear this song."

Jessica Anne "I have often wondered if my current cat Chester could possibly be the reincarnation of my rat Riley. When Riley was getting sick in his old age, I would play him songs from The Beatles his favorite was 'Good Night.' Now whenever Chester is on my lap I play him music while I brush him. He prefers soft classical lol. So anyhow, that Beatles song GN randomly popped into my head (haven't heard the song in years as it was too emotional to listen) and I played it for Chester. For a moment, he just sat and listened. Then he began to close his eyes and purr, a few times putting his arm up on my chest as if to tell me he likes the song too."

Johanan "I was driving back home from work and was thinking about how happy I was because my husband is coming home. Then Katia's and my song started playing... I think it was her letting me know she was happy her Daddy was coming home too".

Johnson wrote: "This morning when I turned on my radio, the song that was 'our song' - Unconditional by Katy Perry was playing. I had been feeling sad having not had any Signs in a while. I had asked him last night to please let me know he's around. I could feel his presence as I got ready for bed and then that song played this morning when I really needed to be reassured."

SOUNDS

Pets will use sounds that are familiar to you as Signs or messages. Many times, I would hear Friend # 1 bark to protect me. He was making sure I was aware of something even when everything was quiet and all the other dogs were nowhere or quiet in plain sight.

You'll also hear animals cleaning fur, drinking water, eating in that old familiar way, rattling their collar or food bowl, scratching and bumping against the floor or furniture. Cats will purr or meow to parents from Rainbow Bridge. Many pet parents report hearing their pet's nails clicking down the hallway or on the den and kitchen floor. Pets will also knock or scratch on and even open doors, set off the doorbells, stir up the wind chimes, and create things that "go bump" to get your attention. Before you feel fear **ASK- Fluffy is that you??** You'll get a reply. If it's not Fluffy then **ASK "who is it" and "what do you want me to know"**!

My horse would neigh, paw, shake her head and nuzzle at her lover "Liberty Blue" (who died of colic) when he would visit her in the barn. **Oftentimes, you'll hear noises of living animals playing with or looking into space as if listening to an "imaginary friend, or barking at absolutely nothing." They are interacting with Pet Spirits.**

Ken and Nella were surprised one night by hearing their Bassett Patrick's tail thumping on the floor by their bed as he did every night before bedtime!

A member wrote "Last week I was lying in bed, and I heard the jingling of a dog collar coming from the other room. It was 5:00am and dead quiet. There was no way it could have been anything else and it was so distinct. It sounded like my Riley when he would scratch and his tags would jingle together."

From Hong Kong Nina wrote "My friend's Dog let my friend know he was visiting by making loud noises by rattling the food bowl and treat container."

Pet Spirits
Never leave your side.
They watch over & sleep with us
because Their Love is Never Ending!

THOUGHTS

Mental perceptions can trigger you to sense your pets living energy is around you. Example, you can be in line at Wal-Mart when all of a sudden you start to cry because you "thought" of your baby. What's happening is that your pet's Spirit is near and touching your heart. Your Soul recognizes they are there which is why you spontaneously respond. The close connection with your beloved pet is what triggers an emotional response.

From Italy Morgana writes: "Hi everybody! I lost my beloved cat 20 days ago, and don't know why I feel calm inside and I miss her only physically. I also have sudden feelings of love, warmth and happiness and a sort of awareness to be in mental contact with her. It's as if it was when she was alive. It's like she is here with me but at the same time I am also there with her."

A: This is an example of the energetic interwoven Heart connection you have with your pet who is a fiber of your life's tapestry.

When the thread representing you and your pet's relationship is "removed" from your heart after they cross over, you feel an empty void. Morgana is using her thoughts to connect with her Cat's Spirit so her Heart and their relationship are now based on her Cat's new connection. Her attitude brings joy -not pain or sorrow.

TRAVEL

Many Pet parents "feel" their fur children with them on trips. Is it possible? YES!!! Unencumbered by a physical body your pet can be anywhere at any time!

UNUSUAL OCCURRENCES

When you are crying nonstop, praying or just wondering if your beloved "family member" is okay, sometimes your pet will cause a commotion or distraction that you recognize in your heart is their response to let you know that they are fine! Deceased pets will bring toys out that you KNOW you stored in a safe place!! Or rearrange desks, brief cases, back packs, suitcases, pocketbooks, containers, shelves, household objects, closet items, bathroom accessories and home décor or garage space that was included in "their" territory just to get your attention. Even hiding things, ASK your pet where they put it. It's just to get YOUR attention!

Since there are no coincidences, you'll drive down a road named after your pet (like Greta in "I'm Home!" a Cat's Never-Ending Love Story") or look up and see a building or business sign with their name, letting you know they are OK.

Maybe you'll be looking in a catalogue for animal beds and all of the samples names are your pet's name, another "Hello, I love you!"

You may get a postcard in the mail or be given a bouquet of flowers with special wording on the card that triggers your heart's knowing that it's a sign from your pet. You're probably correct!

Your pet's signs will be very clear and distinct. Your heart and soul WILL recognize / KNOW it's them!

Sneha shared "Okay so this may look little freaky but I feel this could be a sign. Today being Friday, Mitthu had transitioned on Friday so I tend to get very emotional dealing with it. Anyways, I came home and saw this unusual claw like print on my window. Pls excuse flash reflection on the glass. My in laws are certain there was no bird in the house today. The print is from inside of the house."

A member shared "In Lucky's world, a belch equated to gratitude for having fed her.

While my son and I were talking about Lucky, neither of us were paying any attention to the little teddy bear I had sitting on the end table between our chairs.

I set it there intending to put it back in its proper place eventually. Out of the blue, the little bear burped, my son and I both fell silent.

Now, this was a little bear toy that made random sounds or spoke different phrases (giggling, asking you to rub its tummy, telling you to play with it, etc.) depending upon whether you pushed a specific button.

You HAD to push a button to initiate a response.

You could not trigger this thing by knocking it on the floor, shaking the table or anything of that nature - you had to actually depress the tiny button in its neck or the one in its stomach - a button the size of the tip of a pencil - in order to set it off. Neither my son nor I had touched it. We hadn't even touched the table it was sitting on.

My son and I froze, looking at one another, then at the bear. After a moment or two, when nothing else happened, we began talking again.

Again, the bear burped, followed by a giggle. Seconds later, another burp, then another, followed by another giggle.

By now, my son and I were dumfounded, but we both had the very same thought. 'It's Lucky, and he's trying to tell us thank you for having the strength to let him go.'

The burping, giggling and occasional 'excuse me' continued from this little bear for maybe another 15-20 seconds, and then stopped. I have not been able to trigger that bear to burp since.

Some might say it was coincidence, maybe a malfunctioning battery or a short somewhere in the bear's electronics system. I don't know, maybe they'd be right, maybe there's nothing mystical about the whole incident. To be totally honest, I don't care what anyone else thinks about it. We believe this was Lucky and that he wanted us to know he's okay, and that he's happy. I believe he wanted to thank us, and he did so in a way he knew we'd understand."

Kim's Chippers was a busy boy. Having only one occurrence is not always the case. You can get an ongoing mixture of Signs, Messages and various Visitations!

"Have had several sign from my Chippers the last several days: I found 3 feathers in Popcorn's stall Saturday morning and saw a chipmunk (his namesake) on my way to get my hair done; found a penny at work yesterday and today, found a penny in the parking lot at Safeway while I was at massage therapy, I started thinking of him, saw him sitting on the floor next to the table in my mind's eye (started to cry -- good thing I was face down so didn't have to explain that to my therapist) and when I was getting ready to leave, found 2 dimes and a penny on the floor! He WAS there with me!! I believe he knew just what an AWFUL day I was having!"

Shirley wrote "today is 6 months after Thomas' death. On my way home, a school bus cut in front of me 2 blocks from my house. The brand of school bus was Thomas. My Thomas knows I miss him and was saying hello."

Don't even be surprised if you're fighting, feeling sick, having an intense conversation, in the middle of a business deal or making love and you look up and there is Fluffy or they create a distraction. Pets can also be VERY selfish and demanding of your attention at the most inconvenient times!

He misses that special bond
with the person
           he had to leave behind.

Somewhere in time
we will
begin Again!

VISITATIONS & VISIONS

See How to ask for an Energy Visitation (Vision) on page 83, 88 and Page 93.

Visitations come in three Forms

*an Energy Visitation in which you sense/ feel and recognize their presence but do not see it,
*a quick fleeting Glitter or Sparkler Visitation
*a Visual Visitation (Vision) where you look at and see the Pet Spirit form for an extended period of time.

Orbs are a different distinct form of energy visit.

Personal example: After Mike was killed, he would begin to formulate in glitterized sparkly Spirit form in front of me. I was so emotionally traumatized that I couldn't handle it! I was so scared when he asked to show up i.e. assemble in front of me so I would see him, I didn't allow him to do so.

It is my greatest regret that I did not ask or let Mike present himself as a living energy being, while he was in an energy state capable of assembling into a recognizable form. Many individuals have seen their beloved deceased people or pets' Spirit during a visit. To them it was very comforting and healing. There is nothing to fear and a great deal to learn "face to face." FYI - Most processes of connection and communication are the same with humans or animals.

Anne wrote "Two days after her passing, it was early morning and I was lying in bed when I heard my dog's ears flapping. I thought could this be possible? Well later that morning I was sitting in the living room having coffee when I saw her walk past me."

Sally "it's nice when they pay a Visit. Just 2 nights ago, my new puppy was sleeping on my neck, and then he looked up to the door and jumped out of bed. I thought she wanted to go outside I opened the back door. She kept staring down the hall then went back to the room. We lay back down then I heard the door in the hall way open. My old dog Nina use to always open the door and sleep there. I knew it was her coming by."

OVER IMAGING is a visitation process used by a reincarnated deceased Pet to insure "Mom" knows the new body is housing the original Soul. Sometimes a deceased pet may appear as a "Vision" in steam form and superimpose their old body image over the new reincarnate' s body to insure you understand "it's me again!" A wonderful example is Union Jack in my book **I'm Home!" a Dog's Never-Ending Love Story.**

Leanne shared another Over Imaging Visit: "I just saw the strangest thing. I saw Jessie's original body super-imposed over her current one. She is now 6 months old. Is this her way of showing me who she is, or are my eyes playing tricks on me? It's not like I didn't know already. Just the other day, I looked at him and he looked right at me and it was like, 'CLICK' I saw Jessie, so I said 'hi, Jessie' and he seemed to acknowledge that and we moved on - it felt like I was seeing his Soul. I think she just wanted me to see that she is one and the same, regardless of the body or the color of her feathers."

In my BLOG pet reincarnation, we have lots of informational articles on our Animal Life after Death Blog, we hope you visit and share.

QUESTIONS:

Can other Pets that I had in my past come Visit me? Yes! Any animal or living energy being on the Other Side can choose to visit at any time as an individual or in a group if you allow them to do so.

When live pets are visited by and play with deceased animals' energy, is that a Sign that the pet in Spirit is going to reincarnate? No. It's just a Sign that animals are very intuitively aware of "all there is" and are having fun with their friend's visit.

Do pet's Spirits visit earth and interact with animals they have previously known?

Yes. Animals live by their keen instincts. They are very aware of energies and entities from across the Veils. Often times your earth pet will continue to "play" or interact with the deceased animal's living energy for years! They may growl over the food bowl at an imaginary friend, or bat a paw at a plain air playmate or act as if they are watching or "looking at" something. Sometimes a living pet will not get up on or sleep in a particular place that was once or still is inhabited by the deceased pet's energy.

Do Pet's recognize the energy of their Deceased Friends?

Sharon writes "I picked up Anna's ashes and Buddy immediately jumped into the front seat and buried his head in the bag. Is it possible he knows it is her?"

A: Yes. There is a wonderful Video on the internet about a dog that has an old master who went into the Hospital and died. Then a wheelchair comes out with a lady who just received a heart transplant from the dog's previous owner. The Dog immediately greeted that woman as if he had known her forever.

He had identified his master's Heart in another physical form. Energy is Energy. That is why cats can identify the smell of death (remember the nursing home cat) or dogs can smell disease or bodies under water or notify Epileptics that they are starting to have a seizure or the blood sugar in low in a Diabetic. Pets are constantly sensing and identifying Energy!

WIND CHIMES

I bought a wind chime for my dog Electra, asking her to choose the one she liked. After testing them all, I KNEW which one. Some days when there is no wind, the chimes are singing. I know she's telling me she loves me from the Other Side.

Tim relates "My friends bought me a Wind chime when my dog Billy passed away. I hung it on a tree he loved to hang out under. Every time, I cut the grass it always chimes even with no wind. I always stop and think about my little buddy. Also, I swear the chime always swings and tries to hits me as I pass. I guess that's his way of saying "What's Up!" He always did things to try to get my attention."

Linda Writes "I hung up a wind chime in entryway to the front porch the day I buried my boy. He rings quite often to let me know he's still by my side."

Do Signs, Messages and Visitations mean my Pet is coming back in this lifetime?

If yes, your pet will provide **more and more** obvious and frequent notice that they are on the way!

As an animal approaches relife, the experiences outlined in the previous chapters will gradually lessen as your pet refocuses all of their energy into reassembling for their return!

If your pet is NOT reincarnating they will just "check in" off and on for the rest of your life.

How can you tell the difference?
It's not easy. Use the prayers to ask your pet for clarity. You will hear the answer in your heart.

When your prayers are answered with a "no," the signs and incidents become more sporadic. The signs will be like an old friend's call from time to time over the years. Your heart will inherently know your pet is just checking in and not going to return.

IF my Pet is Coming Back, Could I miss Him?
That's THE number one question.

NO! Nope, no way, no can do, huh uh, NOT!
Absolutely not! and NO!
*****Remember only 30-40% reincarnate to
continue lessons with you. The other stay with you in
Pet Spirit.

Pet Spirits
visit often.
You will see, feel or sense them
in their favorite spots
or during that special time
you shared each day! It's Real!

After Death Signs book by **Brent Atwater**

© Dianne Virga Photographer.

I hope

* this book has illustrated through various examples and testimonies that After Death pet communication and connection with the Other Side is REAL!
* you understand no matter where your Pet's energy is living now, **it IS ALIVE** and **will be a part of your life forever and always!!!**
It has just changed Form.

In your darkest hours after Transition, ASK your pet to communicate and connect with you.

Life after Death & Reincarnation is REAL!!! Just ask Friend, the Dog with my "B" on His Bottom!

Together you begin AGAIN,

Brent Atwater's latest book release

**Lessons from Loved Ones
in Heaven**
How to Continue Never Ending Love!

Brent Atwater

Just Plain Love® Books
*inspiring thoughts that provide smiles, hugs and healing
for every reader's heart!*

Message to Book Clubs, Retail Stores, Professional Associations & Organizations

Ms. Atwater will be delighted to speak with your group over the phone or schedule a presentation or event. Email us at Brent@BrentAtwater.com.

Questions from the Audience

Can an animal be your Soul mate?

The dictionary defines a soul mate as "one of two beings compatible with each other in disposition, point of view, or sensitivity for whom you have a deep affinity." Some believe that a soul mate is a being with whom we have shared other lifetimes. Below are 2 beautiful descriptions that say it all!

A soul mate is:
1. "When we feel safe enough to open the locks, our truest selves step out and we can be completely and

honestly who we are; we can be loved for who we are and not for who we're pretending to be. Each unveils the best part of the other. No matter what else goes wrong around us, with that one person we're safe in our own paradise. Our soul mate is someone who shares our deepest longings, our sense of direction. When we're two balloons, and together our direction is up, chances are we've found the right person. Our soul mate is the one who makes life come to life." -- Richard Bach

2. A being with "whom we feel profoundly connected, as though the communication and communing that take place between us were not the product of intentional efforts, but rather a divine grace. This kind of relationship is so important to the soul that many have said there is nothing more precious in life." --Thomas Moore

Can we have more than one animal soul mate? YES!!! A soul mate is a portion of all you are. That's why you can have several. However, you can only have one Twin Flame which is your EXACT match and your soul's other half!

Sometimes clients will say "My heart tells me he is still here. Would you tell him I love him and miss him so much?"

YOU can tell you pet that you love him and miss him. He has NEVER Left your side and Never stopped loving you. Where you are, he is!

He has just changed forms and can still hear EVERY word and thought you have plus watch and participate in every activity without the burden of a physical body getting in his way!

YOU have to step over the speed bump of believing your pet is dead into understanding that your pet is NOW in a LIVING energy Spirit form! It's just the Fur, finned or feathered suit that is gone.

Do you conduct Animal Communication Readings?

Yes, I love meeting pets and people. It's an honor to see and talk with Pet Spirits so I can comfort and help heal their parent's heart. PLUS, I learn something new every time!

Why is your Reading different from a traditional Animal Communicator's work?

ACs telepathically "talk" to pets by getting mental thoughts/ impressions. Then they interpret those notions into information for you. I look at and have a face to face conversation with your pet's Spirit.

What do you do in a Reading? (YouTube video and Pet Life Radio show on this subject.)

Do you teach classes?
Yes, Animal Reincarnation Communication

I also teach Animal Intuitive Healthcare & Healing - AIH (How to see inside an animal's body to diagnose, treat and heal health issues)

Brent Atwater's
Just Plain Love® Books presents

RESOURCES for Healing your Heart

1. Facebook Pet Group - Ask questions and learn from our discussions in the World's # 1 Pet Loss, Animal life after death, Afterlife Signs Group.

Professional Bereavement Counselor

Frankie Johnson's contact info is on my website.

2. Pet Loss Radio & Podcasts: Show "Alive Again" on Pet Life Radio.

3. Brent Atwater's YouTube TV Show

4. Pet Loss Blog: Share your stories

5. Workshops, Events / Live Q & A Chats

are announced on Brent Atwater's Facebook Page, Group and Website.

6. Live Events: Want an Event in your area-email us!

7. Return from Rainbow Bridge Videos on YouTube & Poems in 10+ languages. Download

to print out YOUR language at
www.BrentAtwater.com

8. Memorial Rainbow Wristband:

Engraved: My Love is Never Ending. I'm coming back to YOU! ™ These can be found on my website.

9. Readings for Rescue™ live Events.

Ms. Atwater uses her Gifts to raise funds for Rescue and Animal welfare organizations. Email us to create an Event.

BRENT *Live!*
ATWATER

Readings for Rescue™
Animal Communication for Animal Welfare
www.brentatwater.com

We have Translators for our Facebook pages, groups, YouTube videos and personal Readings

Brent Atwater's
Just Plain Love® Books presents

Brent Atwater & Friend

Authority on Pet Afterlife Signs, Animal life after
death & Pet Reincarnation. Pioneer and Founder of
Animal Intuitive Healthcare & Healing

Brent Atwater the Animal Medium (and "Friend" her dog with a "B" on his Bottom) is the world's authority on pet loss, animal life after death, Signs and reincarnation. Brent's Readings are filled with very personal information and specific details that captivate clients and global audiences.

Ms. Atwater has the extraordinary Gift to see inside a body to accurately diagnose current and future health issues and to create healing solutions.

At age 5 Brent's intuitive talents were discovered by Duke University's Dr. J B Rhine the founder of ESP in his initial investigations. Ms. Atwater's specialized intuitive diagnostic abilities have earned her the nickname of the "human MRI."

Her world renowned Medical Intuitive practice has highly respected, evidence based, documented and published case studies. Brent can see the organs, nerves, bones, tissue et al inside your body, plus diagnose and predict future events. Therefore Ms. Atwater can determine if and when your pet is going to reincarnate and what they will look like!

Brent's healing work regenerating her dog's spinal cord nerves and vertebra has been documented by

NC State University's School of Veterinary Medicine. She has been a speaker and teacher for the NC Veterinary Association and taught at the New York Open Center. For decades Ms. Atwater has pioneered and founded AIH the field of Animal Intuitive Healthcare & Healing. Her Medical Intuitive Diagnosis MIDI and AIH books are groundbreaking resource books for the science of Medical Intuition and Healing Animals with Integrative Energy Medicine.

In 1987 Brent founded the Just Plain Love®
Charitable Trust. After law school and the death of
her fiancé, Brent refocused her career on helping pets
and their people heal. Ms. Atwater has authored 10
Just Plain Love® Books with more to follow.

Ms. Atwater has devoted decades to researching pet life after death, pet reincarnation and human animal spiritual contracts which produced multiple books whose titles are translated into other languages.

Brent offers us the benefit of her incredible gifts and her passion to help heal and uplift the lives of pets and their people! Her mission is to ignite hope and healing in people and to activate and empower every person's inherent abilities and Gifts.

Ms. Atwater is also a pioneer in healing art medicine by scientifically documenting the healing energy, diagnostic abilities and healing benefits of her Paintings That Heal® (www.BrentAtwater.com). She is one of the contemporary American painters who are bringing forth a new cultural renaissance by blending her classical artistic training with spirituality and energy infused into her healing art.

Brent Atwater's life work facilitates positive and transformative results!

"Friend" is the co-host of Brent's life!

He is a Red tri colored Border collie. Friend
"B"elieves his mission is to expand awareness about
animal reincarnation to help heal hearts. When he's
not assisting Brent with paw signings, pet fund
raising events or practicing hugs and kisses for his
pet therapy work, Friend enjoys being spoiled,
herding fish and turtles in his pond and playing with
his "Mister Bears."

Join Brent Atwater's & Friend's Global Community on, Facebook, YouTube, Twitter Instagram, Pinterest, Periscope, MySpace and others

Just Plain Love® Books

inspiring thoughts that provide smiles, hugs and healing for every reader's heart!

Other Just Plain Love® Titles

Inspirational:

The Beach Book: Beach Lessons for a Workaholic!

Children's Books:

Cancer Kids—God's Special Children!
Cancer and MY Daddy

Life and Spiritual Purpose:

How to Accept, Trust & Live Your Life's Spiritual Purpose: Am I Worthy?
Prayers to Empower Your Life's Spiritual Purpose

Energy Medicine, Intuitive Development:

Medical Intuition, Intuitive Diagnosis, MIDI-
How to See Inside a Body to Diagnose, Treat & Heal
AIH - Animal Intuitive Healthcare & Healing for Veterinarians, Assistants & Technicians

Self Help and Healing, Mind Body Medicine:

Healing Yourself! 23 Ways to Heal YOU!
Lessons from Loved Ones in Heaven, How to Continue Never Ending Love

Brent Atwater's
Just Plain Love® Books presents

Pet Loss, Afterlife, Animal Life after Death
After Death Signs from Pet Afterlife and Animals in Heaven
Conversations with Animals in Heaven
Animal Reincarnation
Animal Life after Death
the Dog with a "B" on His Bottom!
"I'm Home!" a Dog's Never-Ending Love Story
"I'm Home!" a Cat's Never-Ending Love Story
"I'm Home!" a Horse's Never-Ending Love Story
Pet Loss, Afterlife & Pet Life after Death!
La Réincarnation des Animaux de Compagnie
動物は生まれ変わる

CPSIA information can be obtained
at www.ICGtesting.com
Printed in the USA
BVHW090717011118
531456BV00001B/2/P

9 781514 355619